MY BROTHER MY ENEMY

Adrienne Nairn

STENTORIAN
PUBLISHING LTD

STENTORIAN
PUBLISHING LTD

Stentorian Publishing Ltd, 4 Starlight Arcade,
Taupo 3331, New Zealand

First published by Stentorian Publishing Ltd, 2013

Cover design and typesetting by The Art Group
Printed in Hong Kong by Regal Printing Ltd

National Library of New Zealand Cataloguing-in-Publication Data

Nairn, Adrienne, 1948-
My brother my enemy : a true story / Adrienne Nairn.
1. Nairn, Adrienne, 1948- 2. Nairn, Adrienne, 1948- —Family.
I. Title.
920.72—dc 23

ISBN 978-0-473-23781-3

Email for orders or enquiries

adrienne_nairn@yahoo.com

Disclaimer

The contents of this original work must not be taken in any way whatsoever by any
reader as constituting legal advice in relation to the issues it canvasses.
This work has been written solely as a way of understanding the issues. It expresses only
personal views regarding the circumstances in which the author has found herself.
If any reader whosoever considers their circumstances to be in any way similar to those covered
by this book, then they are strongly advised to seek reliable legal advice before undertaking any
remedial legal action.

FOREWORD

I always intended to tell the story of my upbringing in England, my experiences and travels and to record the circumstances of how I came to settle in New Zealand. I wanted to do so for future generations for, all too often, family history is lost upon one's passing. As a consequence, future generations know little of what has gone before.

Over the years I have transcribed autobiographies for others which has made me realise everyone has a story to tell, regardless of whether they think they have led an uninteresting or uneventful life.

This was always something I had intended to do later, rather than sooner. Maybe I saw it as an undertaking which could wait for my twilight years.

However, the events of autumn 1999 led me to undertake what has, to be frank, been a significant mission, much sooner than I had originally contemplated.

In my life, I have always endeavoured to do the best by people, following the age-old edict of 'do as you would be done by'. I have always been the one to say sorry. If someone walks into me in the street, it is me who says sorry. It comes naturally, even if I am not at fault.

But on one occasion I did not say sorry. That action landed me in trouble and has brought me thirteen years of turmoil and family strife.

There are no text books on how to live life or how to deal with particular problems. We are all brought up differently. We have different standards and we act in a different manner, even if we are from the same family.

Others may have dealt with my situation in a completely different way, but I made my own choices. Members of my family, particularly my only brother Michael, have made their choices.

Throughout my life, I have also always told people how I feel, what I am going to do, or what I have done. I feel that is only fair and I prefer to be open and honest with everyone. That's my personal creed. However, if I am asked to keep a secret, I do so, religiously. There are reasons people keep secrets and these are usually centred on the desire to not offend others or cause them grief.

My brother, Michael, has never been open about his actions. He is devious and cunning and I remain unsure to this day why he turned against me when he did. I have been left wondering, is it all really just down to money and greed?

This book is an account, on the basis of evidence I have collected and information I can prove, of what is commonly seen among families. It is a personal story of family strife, caused by a dispute over the proceeds of an estate, in this instance, that of our step-mother.

My preference would have been to have settled this matter amicably and in the nature of the close relationship I once had with my older sibling. But for the reasons outlined in this book, I now know this is no longer possible.

My second choice would have been to have this disturbing matter settled in a Court of Law. Regrettably, that is where most family disputes over money and wills end up, in the absence of common sense and logic.

My decision not to take this costly and destructive course has been prompted by a number of considerations. There is the older generation to think about. Fortunately my father did not live to see the horrendous outcome of his generosity, but my mother is still alive and watching from the sidelines. She has become a pawn in the game my brother decided to play.

Michael could have stopped this affair at any time, but it seems to me his military background would not allow him to do that. I am sure he is inclined to the view that he has to win, no matter the cost.

My intention has always been to try to resolve what has become a prolonged dispute between siblings by any means possible. I went to mediation to try to settle it, but my brother decided not to abide by the agreement we had reached. If he had done so, this matter would have been closed and this book would have been an autobiography of a vastly different style, as was my original intention.

There are many reasons I feel the need to tell this story. Principal among them is that I cannot let my brother defame my father, who is not here to defend himself. I also owe this to my daughter and her sons, all of whom should now be benefiting from a sizeable inheritance. That they are not able to do so, I view as despicable.

Beyond the immediate confines of my own family, this is a story that needs to be told because it involves the way British society, indeed many societies throughout the world today, operate.

It will be obvious to anyone reading this that like many before me,

I have come up against the old boys' network, in the guise of the Police, the Masons, local authorities, solicitors, barristers, Ombudsmen and even charities set up to defend the aged. None of them, it seems, have been there to uphold the law.

If my story can make a difference to the way complaints of this nature are handled by the authorities, then something good will have come from it.

The story I am telling involves a mammoth waste of resources - one that has spread from one country at the top of the world to another at the bottom. Many hours have been expended for no purpose, with the cost to the Police and local authorities involved being significant. The cost has, in reality, been on the public, as they pay the officials who have played a part in this travesty of justice.

I am strongly of the view that if my brother had told my step-mother to come to her senses years ago this family dispute would never have arisen. If the Police had told my brother to adopt a more sensible, reasoned and reasonable attitude, so much of their time would not have been wasted, as it most surely has been.

In writing this book, I am making a strong plea for the law to be changed to protect the elderly from unscrupulous people preying upon them. Such a law change needs to involve an extensive and comprehensive investigation into the way powers of attorney can be used, and often are, to the detriment of those who provide them.

My parting thought is that if I can leave this world knowing I have made a difference to the lives of those who find themselves in similar circumstances, often through no fault of their own, then my struggles will not have been in vain.

Adrienne Nairn
Taupo, New Zealand
04 April 2013

DEDICATION

To my dear grandsons Evan and Curtis for making my life such a joy, bringing laughter instead of tears. You are the future and I love you.

ACKNOWLEDGEMENTS

To my cherished husband Ian, who has always been there as a calming influence - one who knew the truth from the very beginning and told me never to trust my brother. Regrettably, I did not heed his words of infinite wisdom. Had I done so, the outcome may have been vastly different. But isn't hindsight a wonderful thing?

Also to Rachel, another who always knew the truth. Although only 14 at the time my father and step-mother gifted the monies and finding herself ten years later embroiled in this debilitating matter from the outset, she never wavered in her belief that truth and justice will prevail. And latterly to her lovely husband, Jamie, who has always been supportive of my efforts and those of his wife. We will try to secure Tom Cruise to play you in the movie.

To Anna my soul mate and confidante. Who needs counsellors when you can go to lunch with Anna?

To Peggy and Heather, my two very dear friends, who gave their support when it was most needed - particularly at that horrendous mediation session in 2010 - and who turned my days in Exeter from horror into a most memorable time, full of fun and laughter.

To Mike and Sheila who were, most fortunately for me, in England in 2008 and acted as taxi drivers and advisers, providing a much-needed life-line.

To Mike H, always willing to act as a courier, confidant and friend, assisting in any way he could.

And to Catherine (Oggy) who reminded me of stories of school life and who brought back many happy memories.

To Ted Farmer, who has been there for me, writing numerous letters and emails in support of my cause, backing my endeavours to get to the truth, and contacting my brother and the Police in a bid to see that this family matter was brought to a logical and sensible conclusion, as it should have been a long time ago. My gratitude will always be with Ted.

Despite what others in my family may assert, I have many friends, who have listened, offered advice or just been there for me. There are too many to list, but I want you all to take this as a personal acknowledgement. You all mean so much to me.

To Leo Hunter, my McKenzie friend, a total stranger who took on the enormous task of sorting through the reams of paperwork, believing in me and finally publishing the digital version of my original work.

To Mark and his team at The Art Group, in my home town of Taupo, in the very centre of the North Island of New Zealand, home of the Great Lake. Your design excellence is reflected in the pages of this hard copy edition, and I am thankful for the enthusiasm and professionalism you have shown in getting this work into print.

And to Chris Birt, another stranger who took me at face value, who believed in my story and who provided invaluable guidance during the transformation of this book, from its former life as a digital edition to its current format. The lengthy investigation undertaken by Chris into a famous double murder cold case in New Zealand and his latest book, All The Commissioner's Men, has inspired me to stand up for what I believe in and to refuse to be a victim. Chris has worked tirelessly on the reconstruction of the original manuscript, published digitally as Scuppering the Boat, and has questioned and tested my words when and where needed. His professional editing skills, acquired over four decades, have resulted in a work I am both happy with, and proud of.

PROLOGUE

Last night I dreamt my brother was murdering me – again. This was not in the physical sense, you understand. He is much too clever for that. He has connections, you see.

Sometimes my dream involves a savage mugging on a very dark night. Sometimes it is an attack in broad daylight. But occasionally an enraged driver runs me down when I am walking alone.

Then there is the dream that someone tampers with my car, causing me to crash.

Is this a premonition, or merely the wanderings of a disturbed mind? I often wonder.

PART ONE

~ *One* ~

They say that everything happens for a reason. However, even now, I struggle to understand the reasoning behind what happened to our family.

Like most ignorant people, I struggled to make sense of the law where admissible evidence does exist, despite having worked in several solicitors' offices. This was so much so that naïve dreams of everlasting love turned into a nightmarish fear of my life as the moment came for me to decide which version of common sense to heed, and apply, after I realised I was being groomed as a victim of creative ambiguity. In an almighty flash, I recall a quite rare moment of indecision as I started to fight hard against the sensation of drowning in murky waters of creative deceit.

Exposing that flash to reasoning, I really don't know why my father married my mother. He had had previous romances, even being engaged to another woman. On that occasion, I understand the proposal came from the woman in question, but I believe she broke off the engagement when she got the ring. Of course, she kept it.

My father had another romance, with a nurse called Jenny. That seemed to be really serious, but their jobs, during the Second World War, conspired to keep them apart.

What I do know though is why my mother married my father. She was a nurse in Edinburgh at the time but she hated nursing. As a junior probationer she had to undertake all the menial tasks. The excitement promised by war was something quite different, something that attracted her in an instant.

At the time my father was based in Bridlington, between Hull and Scarborough on the English East Coast. That is where they met, at a round of parties the locals so enjoyed, entertaining the troops. The 24th Lancers were due to leave Bridlington for France, but as my father's autobiography reveals, his future mother-in-law very hastily intervened.

Grandmother Allen, as she became to me upon my birth some years later, was a very strict lady who simply oozed the airs to match. She was also a snob, considering herself to be above everyone else.

Before his embarkation on the voyage across the Channel which was to be his undoing in more ways than one, Mrs Allen summoned my father to her house. Her daughter Joyce, otherwise known as José, was well out of his sight on my father's entry.

'Now I hear you are moving away,' Grandmother Allen declared. My father was really shocked. 'Even if I knew such a thing, I could not confirm or deny,' he answered guardedly, aware that civilians were not supposed to know about troop movements before the fact. It was, and still is, a serious offence in the eyes of the Army hierarchy for any soldier to disclose their troop movements – unless they are ordered to – and that is particularly the case in times of war.

Not to be out-manoeuvred, this assertive lady declared: 'You don't have to. I know all about it. But Mr Allen and I want you to do something regarding José before you go.'

My father responded, truthfully, that he had not thought seriously about the matter under discussion at that moment.

Rather haughtily, but still with a smile, the older lady observed he should obviously think enough of José not to let her go back to emptying bed pans in Edinburgh.

'You will never want for anything if you marry her, I can promise you that,' she declared, adopting the stance of offering more of a carrot than a stick. 'Have a think about it, but let us know.' With that she swept from the room, leaving my father really quite stunned. But just as she did so, José entered, leaving him to contemplate what appeared to be rather astute timing.

Some days later my father visited Mr Allen to express his concern about the prospect of marriage when it was possible that he could be killed in the war. Although ill himself at that time, Mr Allen did not show any concern and he was certainly not opposed to my father becoming his son-in-law. So my father and my mother became engaged, eventually marrying in March 1944. My father's best man was Sir Robert Arbuthnot, a Baronet, and a choice which very much thrilled his newly-acquired snobbish mother-in-law.

Although touch and go, due to leave perhaps not being granted, the wedding passed without a hitch, which was just as well really as Grandmother Allen was not an understanding woman and would have made that clear had her plans for this big day in her life been ruined.

My mother was just 19 when she married, 11 years my father's junior. That is quite an age difference and they really didn't know each other well.

To his horror my father realised, at some point during the honeymoon, he had married a child – one whose only conversational input took the form of keen, simplistic monosyllabic replies. It was not long before Maurice Lobb considered his marriage to José Allen to have been a mistake, driven by what he saw as the need to be my mother's husband, father, mother, brother and sister, all rolled into one.

Just three months after their marriage my father took part in the D-day landings in early June 1944. While those events were to signal the end of the war in Continental Europe, my father did not escape unscathed, returning to England with a bullet and shrapnel in him. He was lucky to survive, but while he was never active in that horrendous conflict again, he was always so proud of the fact he fought and was wounded for his country. He recorded in the foreword to his autobiography his sentiments about this period of hardship, when the world was at war and when so many families experienced such tragedy.

> To my dear grandchild, Rachel, and any who may come after her. When I look at our family tree, it grieves me to see how few cousins you have and, indeed, none on my side of the family at this time. No-one can tell you of the struggle through generations to ensure you have more security, more chance in life, better things such as education, comforts and more pleasures than my generation and those before me ever had. Remember these people with pride and gratitude for their dedication and determination, pioneer spirit and devotion and the fact their efforts have left much for your enjoyment and future.

I remember an incident relating to the pride my father felt at the actions in which he had been involved, along with many of his friends and fellow soldiers. It happened when I was quite young, in the days when they still played the national anthem at the cinema once the film had ended, aimed at instilling patriotism into the public. On this particular occasion my father and I stood steadfast, as was expected. But some of the patrons began to walk out.

This appeared to be an instant irritant to my father and he moved into the aisle and stood in front of one man menacingly who had to stop and stand still too. I was of course acutely embarrassed, but Dad was a proud Royalist – one prepared to die to uphold his beliefs.

My father was, however, determined to make the marriage work and the newly-weds set up home in a modest, but nice little house, in Hounslow.

Unfortunately nothing he chose by way of furnishings was anywhere near good enough for Mrs Allen and soon parcels and packages began to arrive on the doorstep from Allens, the family business owned and operated by my grandfather. Carpets, curtains, sheets, clothes and a variety of other quality goods arrived through a constant stream of 'gifts' as my grandfather put it when my father eventually cornered and quizzed him. Being the proud man he was, my father insisted on paying for it all, even though he hadn't asked for any assistance, and often he ended paying more than he could afford.

As mentioned earlier, my mother came from a well-to-do family. Her parents were Richard Allen and his wife Madeleine Allen whose maiden name was Woodmansey. Granny Allen – the one and same who had captured my father in the lounge room encounter – was very strict. She was certainly not a loving kind of person like my other grandmother, Granny Lobb, as I called her.

I can only remember one nice thing my maternal grandmother said about me and it has stuck in my mind all my life. 'This child has lovely thick hair,' she observed. To me that was praise indeed.

Other than that I know little of the Woodmansey family line. I do know, however, that Granny Allen had two brothers, one of whom she did not get on with at all. In my view, she was a snob who simply loved to think she was above everyone else – and she acted accordingly.

My grandfather, Richard Allen, had a brother Charles, and two sisters, Lily and Clara. The sisters were spinsters who lived together. I remember being taken to visit them as a child. They lived in a dark, dreary house but they were sweet enough. Aunt Lily was large and fat and Aunt Clara, thin and spindly. The latter wore her hair in two plaits coiled up and pinned around her ears like the stereotypical matron.

I vaguely remember Uncle Charles working in the family business, along with grandfather Richard. Charles had three children, Margaret, Judy and John. But my mother did not appear to have a good relationship with those cousins. I only ever remember her saying quite nasty things about them.

Allens, the family enterprise, was primarily a furriers and as such was frequented by the elite of Bridlington, especially the grand, well-to-do ladies who would come and buy the very best of furs there. Some came from afar to shop at Allens, as it was a well-known up-market store. I say 'store' because it was more than a furriers, being four storeys high and having a four-person lift, complete with an ever-helpful attendant.

Upon entry, those shopping at Allens would be secured by two grills being drawn across by the lift attendant, always a man. He pressed all the buttons, having asked if his passengers were going up or down. Lingerie was on the top floor, haberdashery on the second floor, ladies' fashions and furs on the first floor and at ground level, jewellery, carpets and curtains prevailed. It was a scene, as I remember it, straight from the television programme Are You Being Served? That programme came decades later of course. The characters of that very entertaining television series were replicated. Miss Lindsay was 'Mrs Slocombe', complete with purple hair, Mr Yelland was 'Captain Peacock' and Val was 'Mr Lucas'.

On my father's side of the family were my grandmother Adah and grandfather John Lobb, who was known as Jack. To me, they were absolutely wonderful, down-to-earth, honest people. They had no airs and graces – unlike my maternal grandmother – and I loved them dearly.

Grandmother Adah was one of 16 children, but I didn't know any of her brothers and sisters. I remember my grandfather Jack's two sisters, Maud and Muriel. They were also spinsters who lived in another dark dreary house, but in Devon.

My father would sometimes take me to visit, and one of my earliest memories is of Aunt Maud telling me the bogey man would come to get me if I continued to suck my thumb. I then heard a knocking the moment she said it. I was terrified and it took me years to work out it was Aunt Maud knocking underneath the table. This aunt was a very strict disciplinarian, having been a school teacher all her life.

My father had one sister, Marjorie. Their relationship was not very good and I believe they did not speak for years. The cause of this sorry state of affairs appears to have had its origin in the fact that Marjorie married one of my father's best friends. For a reason of which I am not aware, my father did not take too kindly to that.

However, I'm pleased to say our grandmother made a huge effort to ensure we had a good relationship with Marjorie and her daughter, Valerie, my first cousin. Whenever we were left in her charge, Granny Lobb took the opportunity to arrange meetings with them. I am so glad she did, because I had a great relationship with my Aunt Marjorie until she died and still have that with Valerie who is not only a cousin, but a wonderful friend also. I am godmother to her daughter Debbie.

My mother had two siblings. Her older brother, Richard, married Judy and they had three children, Nicholas, Susan and Caroline. My father, in his wisdom, orchestrated a job for Richard in Sible Hedingham, where we lived at the time. Richard was a doctor and he was able to provide support for my mother, who was by then struggling with married life, two children – Michael and I – and her role as a housewife.

My Aunty Judy was my godmother, while my mother's sister, Ruth, and her brother, Uncle Richard filled that traditional role for Michael. Uncle Richard was a lovely man. He kept bees and had a huge embarrassing laugh. When I was 15, my mother, Judy, Susan and I went to Paris for a holiday. We had a lovely time, but on our return, just as Mother began recounting our adventure to my grandparents she slowly realised Grandfather Allen was wearing a black tie. 'What is wrong?' she asked.

The news that Uncle Richard had died, suddenly of a heart attack, while we were away enjoying ourselves came as a bombshell. My mother always blamed Judy for Richard's death, insisting that he had worked too hard – all his medical duties, as well as a lot of the housework, cooking, and looking after the children, a thoroughly modern man.

Ruth was my mother's younger sister. She was considered to be the pretty, frivolous one, very much the fun girl. As a young girl during the war she ran away from her boarding school with two airmen and was later found in their barracks, or so the story goes. She later married Trevor Green, a solicitor in the town, and they had two daughters, Sally and Madeleine.

The marriage between my father and mother didn't last long, despite his pledge to strive hard to make it work. Looking back, I don't actually have any memory of my parents living together and just when they stopped cohabiting is unknown to me.

I can remember living in Crawley Down and my father keeping pigs and chickens. One of the pigs was our pet called Snowy who followed us around and it was rather a sad day when I got home to find he had 'gone to market'. Even before I was five years old, I knew what that meant!

After years of struggling, my mother eventually walked out on my father, arriving on the doorstep of Granny and Grandpa Allen with two children in tow. I was five or six at the time, with my brother Michael almost three years older. My grandparents took us in and we lived with them for a while.

Much later my brother told me Mother had an affair with the

milkman. I don't know for certain it was actually the milkman, but I am aware that she was in a relationship with a man called Mayer before she parted company with my father. My father, it seems, was not privy to that knowledge.

Mother's ploy was to encourage my father to go out to target-shooting practice. It was his hobby at the time, and each shoot would take up several hours of his time. As soon as Dad had left, she would then phone Mayer from a telephone box to let him know the coast was clear.

Occasionally Granny Lobb looked after us. On these occasions we would travel with our mother by train and on arrival at the station she would deliver us into that kindly old lady's arms, before getting back on the train to go to London 'for a day of shopping'.

But one thing my Granny noticed was that she never got back into the same carriage we had alighted from. It was usually the next one, and in that carriage always the same man would be waiting.

Eventually, it all came out, as this type of clandestine encounter almost always does. But the informant was somewhat unexpected, being Mayer's own sister. She knew this was a fact and she also knew that Grandmother Allen occasionally joined my mother and Mayer for outings.

My father was of course astounded by the revelation that he had an unfaithful wife, but I am unaware of what part that played in the ultimate demise of their marriage. What I do know is that Mayer's sister was so incensed by what had been going on that she said she was prepared to bear witness in the divorce proceedings to that effect.

Divorce was not so common in those days and there was quite a lot of stigma attached to such proceedings. To avoid prolonged agony and embarrassment, Mother was instructed by Granny Allen and her solicitor to apply quickly for divorce on the grounds of mental cruelty but when she turned up at Court in York with my Granny Allen and her sister Ruth in tow and saw Mayer's sister was present, more than willing to bear witness against her brother, new divorce terms were suggested, with my father then proceeding to divorce my mother on the honest grounds of adultery. But the Allens got their revenge, forcing my father to part with all his belongings and the matrimonial house, based on the premise that everything had been loaned to him and my mother by Allens, the family business.

My father could not resist, although of course he knew he had been diligently repaying his in-laws for the multitude of gifts that had arrived from the family store without his prior agreement or consent. Of course no receipts were ever issued.

My grandparents bought my mother a bungalow and set her up with duties in their business, working from the bottom up – or in this case the top to the bottom as far as the Allens' store layout was concerned. From lingerie, on the top floor, she worked her way through the various departments until she ended up in the office on the ground floor and in time, she got to run the business.

Although my father was granted access, I missed him terribly, and I think my brother did too. It was not an easy situation for him, or for us. Bridlington was a long way from Sussex, but he would often drive up to Grantham, which was then deemed to be half way, where our mother handed us over. A number of times, I remember our father driving all the way to Bridlington – up and back in a day – just to take us out to lunch.

~ *Two* ~

My big brother, Michael, was born in 1945 in Bridlington. I remember thinking he was a particularly nasty boy on two occasions. Once when we were walking home together from primary school he looked deep into some bushes. Scaring hell out me, he suddenly yelled 'snake! Run!' Witless, I ran as fast as my little legs would carry me, believing the snake was coming to get me. Yet he sauntered on behind casually. In hindsight, it is unlikely there was ever a snake, but Michael delighted in frightening me, a precursor to what was, many years later, to come perhaps?

On another occasion, Michael cut my hair up one side, leaving the other as it was. Remedial action had to be quickly taken by our mother.

Those incidents aside, we actually got on really well during our childhood, playing games on the beach, annoying golfers on the nearby golf course and venturing deep into the fields of a nearby farm. It was all good kids' stuff really, when he was around.

My mother was always after my father for maintenance payments he just didn't have most of the time, although he always paid for what and when he could. On one occasion she tried to have him arrested, but when he explained to police he just did not have the money they realised the futility of it all. I know he was always frugal with food and I was quite horrified to see him eating bread and dripping, and I know at one time he only took a mere £3 a week from the business to live on.

At the age of 11 Michael was sent to Archbishop Holgate's boarding school in York. The Allen grandparents paid, of course!

Later, upon reading one of his early reports from boarding school days, the notation observed that 'Michael is settling down well, we hope.' That was rather ominous because he was not.

Michael ran away several times, heading to my father. Once, during one of his scampering exercises, I remember police knocking on our door in the middle of the night. This reduced Mother to a state tears, sitting on my bed, crying helplessly. That happened at least twice and he was eventually expelled by that school as a result.

This led to my father gaining custody of Michael. That was odd at the time because Courts rarely, if ever, awarded custody to fathers when they were divorced, no matter how cruel the mothers were.

My brother told me in later years that he had spent his formative years with our father. He really enjoyed camping in particular. He used to go from East Grinstead with the Boy Scouts to Ashdown Forest and loved it.

He remembered his two Scout masters at East Grinstead. Both had a tremendous impression on him and he certainly got the feel for outdoor life in the woods and camping and things like that.

Much later, when Michael joined the Special Air Services and did a sniping course he thought the instructions weren't as sound as those he had in the Scouts.

At some stage Michael was involved in petty crime – stealing and the like. He was caught, and presumably both parents were at a loss as to what to do with him. I remember my father telling me later that Michael had gone into the Army because the only other choice was to be sent to borstal.

As Michael was living with my father, I was mostly brought up alone in Bridlington. It was a seaside town and I was regularly reminded by my grandmother how lucky we were to be living in such a lovely place. More than once she reminded me that other children would love to have the opportunity to play on the beach every day. We did enjoy it, along with the seaside activities of course – if we were allowed to experience them. But we were certainly not permitted to go to the amusement arcades.

We always went to the musical shows at the Spa Hall and the Pavilion, which were held in the summer season; but in our eyes Bridlington only seemed to attract the B-Listers. However one wonderful summer Adam Faith came for the season. What a coup for Bridlington! We hung around the stage door hoping to see him, or at least his backing group, the Roulettes, and we were rewarded for our patience.

The family had a beach hut down on Pitts Wall in the summer season. It was always number 14, the last in line before the grassed area. This allowed us to spread out on to the open space at the side. We would go down loaded up with picnics. The deck chairs, rugs, kettle, buckets and spades were stored in the hut, and we children were told to go off and play. Of course we went without question to dig deep into our independently-childish world, having loads of fun in the process.

We enjoyed building sea walls with the sand, hoping that if we built one high enough it would stop the tide coming in. Of course it never did! But we would hold out as long as we could and once the sand wall broke, we would climb up the stone wall to safety as the water burst through. We liked to walk along to where the donkey rides were and help out by leading these loyal little animals, hoping to get a free ride at the end of it.

Of course we always swam in the sea and the one thing I will say about my Granny Allen is that, despite being in her sixties, she would often swim with us. I'm that age now, and there is no way you would get me into the North Sea, even in the mid-summer.

It was certainly great to have the beach hut to come back to and be able to change in comfort.

These were care-free, fun-filled days and I remember them well, being a child in a child's world, before the onset of my teenage years. In those days we often went on family picnics with our cousins, the Greens, to the little village in Yorkshire called Goathland. Later it became famous as the fictional village of Aidensfield for Heartland, the hugely-popular television series set in the 1960s.

We would all go to the Dales National Park, always stopping at Thornton le Dale for coffee. But rather than buying from the cafés, we took our own and drank from a thermos sitting under the horse chestnut trees. It was nice having a natural canopy to shade from the sun when it dared to show its face.

In the Dales we had our own "spot" walking a fair distance, crossing a stream with rugs and our picnic hampers. This was great fun.

But family holidays were not really the norm for me. When other children went away with their parents and grandparents, I would go and visit my father, spending most of my time with him while he worked at his hardware shop. I particularly liked going out with him when he made his deliveries.

When I became older, my mother stopped handing me over at Grantham and I was put on a train in Hull by myself, with my father picking me up at Kings Cross in London. I always travelled on the Pullman, the last of the big glory trains in England. In those days each carriage had a steward and I was left in his or her care. It was comfortable travelling and we sat at tables either for four or two, where luncheon was served. I just loved it.

Other than staying with my father during the holidays, I also went on school trips. Pen friends were very much the norm in those days and we engaged in exchange holidays.

I went to the Continent with school groups, the reason being that it would give us a chance to practice our German or French. I don't think I spoke one word, but the families I stayed with were lovely and they took me out and about a lot.

Elfie from Austria was my first exchange, then Heidi from Heidelberg. We reciprocated and Elfie and Heidi then came to stay with us. Mother was good at showing them around in the car. Then there was Michelle who lived in Paris. We were older by that time, and I certainly enjoyed my time in Paris. Michelle came back to stay in Bridlington one summer. She was very fond of the English boys and a great laugh. We had a good summer. My Allen cousins came up and I had a French pen friend come and stay too, a lad named Gerard who was in the French Navy.

I can only ever remember taking one holiday with my mother while I was young. My grandfather would never travel abroad. Indeed, I don't think he ever took a day off from Allens. But my grandmother loved travelling and she and Mother would go off to all sorts of places. It suited them both and it certainly suited my mother as my grandmother always paid.

On just one occasion I was invited. We went to Palma in Majorca, but it was not a great success, so I never went with them again. At thirteen years of age, I would rather have been meeting other youngsters, especially boys. But that was definitely frowned upon. After that ill-fated trip to Majorca, if it was term time, I was farmed out to friends, never to my Aunty Ruth and cousins nor to my grandfather.

Granny and Mother then found a new interest, going on cruises, and one certain ship seemed to become their very firm favourite. I soon found out why – my mother had struck up a friendship with one of the officers. This interest continued, but as often happens, things went badly awry. On one cruise Mother intended to surprise the man who had often entertained her. But this voyage was to be her last on that ship I think, as the officer had decided to take his wife along for that trip!

~ *Three* ~

It was the days of the 11+ and I passed. This meant I could go to the Bridlington High School for Girls, rather than the Comprehensive.

I was actually given the choice of going away to boarding school, but with my brother's track record that wasn't a very attractive proposition to me and I declined.

I settled into the High School at the start of the new school year, but as it was a lot further I couldn't walk there, as I had done to Hilderthorpe Primary. On fine days I rode my bike and on the really wet days Mother would take me and a friend in her car, the little Mini bought for her by my grandparents.

It was thought my two cousins, Sally and Madeleine, would follow in their mother's footsteps and go to the High School too. That was not to be. My brother had the opportunity to go to a private school, but he blew it. I had declined the option but there was no reason Sally and Madeleine should not be given the same opportunity. I remember Mother saying Aunty Ruth had kept things quiet on the private school front.

Unbeknown to us, Sally took an entrance exam to Roedean School, and she passed, so she went there as a boarder. It had been widely reported that Princess Anne would be going to boarding school the same year and as Roedean was the top Girls' School at the time it was expected she would be enrolled there. My mother rather nastily suggested this was why my aunt chose that particular school for her elder daughter. However Princess Anne went to Benenden and perhaps my aunt's plans for a Royal friendship for her daughter were thwarted.

Madeleine then followed Sally to Roedean. But she hated it for far different reasons and I believe she was eventually asked to leave.

I was by no means a good student at high school. Sometimes I was bottom of the class and sometimes in the middle. School was okay, but I would not describe my years there as being extraordinary.

I think most people remember their school teachers and I certainly do. Mother and Aunty Ruth had both been to Bridlington High and some of the teachers were still there from their day. The students were all girls and most of the teachers were also female, with only four men I can remember.

My best friend at high school was Catherine, who was more commonly known as Oggy. I was Lobby.

Schools were much stricter then than they are now and uniforms were just that, uniforms. We all wore the same. Skirt lengths had to touch the ground when kneeling. Our hair had to be tied back if longer than shoulder length and if one was caught not wearing their hat anywhere out of school there was trouble. It was said authoritatively that all students represented the school and they had to be recognised in public as doing so.

Committing a misdemeanour or two could – and often would – result in a student being reported, and that would spell trouble.

Occasionally there were petticoat inspections. No frills were allowed. Then we had to wear thick Lisle stockings with a seam up the back. Those seams always had to be straight, or else. As a student, you represented the school after all!

One Saturday I persuaded Oggy to go into a café which was frequented by youngsters. There was a counter by the window and patrons could sit up and have a drink, and be seen from outside. There seemed no harm in that, but at school Oggy was spoken to by Miss Heafford, her form mistress. 'Catherine,' she said, 'I was very disappointed to see you in that café on Saturday. I would have expected it of Adrienne, but not of you!'

I was astounded. It was not a school day and we were merely having a girlish chin-wag, and a drink in full view of the general public, just watching the world go by through the window. Oggy told me later Miss Heafford felt she wanted to keep her on the straight and narrow, as she saw it, encouraging her to work hard to gain university entrance, which she did.

I only got detention once and though I regarded it as unfair, I knew there had to be discipline. The incident leading to this punishment came about because one schoolmaster was a rather weak character although I thought he was lovely. Some of the girls used to 'take the Mickey' but one day it got totally out of hand, and a few of the girls really gave him hell. He was reduced almost to tears. Unlike her male counterpart, our form mistress, Mrs Terry, was made of much sterner stuff. She was absolutely furious when she heard what had happened, claiming we had all abused the male teacher's good nature. Some had of course, but not all. That did not however prevent the whole form from getting detention for the acts of a few.

Most of us loved Mrs Terry and we were all devastated when her bridegroom died of a heart attack on their wedding day. It was so sad.

Our music teacher, Miss Branscombe, told us not a single teacher or prefect wanted to take our form for anything because they considered us to be so naughty. But she stuck up for us because she said we had such lovely voices.

I liked sports but I was not brilliant in this arena. Oggy maintained we were slaves to hockey and lacrosse in the lunch hour. We had two gym and games mistresses, Killer (Miss Kilham) and Miss Kent, both of whom were quite popular.

I remember one time we had a relief gym teacher who knew me because her family was quite friendly with mine. I hated the lessons when she was in charge, because I felt, as she was new, mine was the only name she knew. So it was always 'legs not straight, Adrienne! Come on Adrienne! Get a move on Adrienne!'

Mostly we had a huge respect for our teachers because they were dedicated to their profession, particularly the older spinsters. Most of them would shop at Allens and were therefore friendly with my mother and grandmother. One of them Miss Brearley, lived across the road from us and if she was in the garden and we walked past, my mother would stand and chat, much to my horror. We were more in awe of our teachers then than now.

School lunches were an experience. On a Friday, we were always given fried fish and semolina. Then there was spam in batter. It was quite disgusting and the smell made me feel quite ill. I dislike liver to this day. But the shepherd's pie was very good, as were the assorted puddings, jam roly-poly, treacle sponge and custard. We also had the opportunity to purchase Chelsea buns, iced buns or Bath buns at break times and these were always lovely – fresh and squidgy.

Some girls had crushes in the context of having older pupils to look up to. Oggy had a huge crush on the Milner twins – two for the price of one! I was her lookout and had the job of passing notes if either of them should appear. When the Milner twins left, Oggy transferred her affections to Noreen.

Speaking of crushes, in the modern sense, Mother was not short of admirers of course. A very long string of gentlemen turned up on the doorstep. They included Trevor, Mike, and Anthony, the latter being a psychiatrist. I remember once during a visit by my brother Michael, Anthony engaged him in conversation while waiting for our mother to get ready for their date. Michael sat there making hangmen's nooses, putting them over his finger and then pulling tight with a jerk. I think it was an attempt, by Michael, to provoke Anthony into questioning his behaviour and concluding that he was somewhat mad, but I don't think it worked.

Ron was Mother's favourite though. He was a sales representative for Allens, and he took her out a lot. One day he announced that he was moving to America and I believe Mother expected a marriage proposal, but it never came.

By then Dad had remarried. I quite liked Phyll, his second wife. We had a nice time when I visited, but Michael certainly did not like her and made life very difficult for Dad. What part that played in ending the marriage, if any, I do not know, but it did not last. All of a sudden Phyll was gone.

In Bridlington there was a ritual to life. It consisted of school, holidays – and Allens. My mother worked six days a week so on Saturdays I would often go to the cinema with friends. We loved that, with a good selection of films or cartoons. I particularly remember Flash Gordon which was shown in episodes to entice patrons back the next week. If it was not a day at the cinema, I spent Saturdays doing homework, in which case I would always go and meet my mother for lunch. I would walk into Allens. It was a very imposing store, very large window space and then a long corridor past the lift and the jewellery counter (and Miss Lindsay) to the office. I could usually hear Mother's voice as soon as I walked in the front door. That is not to say she had a loud voice, but it did carry. Everyone would say hello as I walked the length of the shop. Sometimes I would stop to look at new items, always ignoring the 'Do not touch' signs, simply because I could. To this very day I can't help touching things which do not need to be touched.

For Saturday lunch we would always go to the same place, the Lounge Café. Once settled in we would always have the same thing - tomato soup, and toasted teacake.

After lunch if my mother was doing the wages I would go and help, adding up long columns of figures for her. That was something I was quite good at. There was no such thing as calculators in those pounds, shillings and pence days and no cash was handled on the shop floors. There were chutes from every department, with the cash or cheque being put in a container and sent, via the chutes, to the office where they dealt with the proceeds of each sale. If any change was required the money would be sent back using the chutes once more. It was a laborious task which could certainly never be followed today.

There were certainly benefits being a part of the Allens' family retail empire. From my point of view, the benefit came in the form of clothes. As I got older I actually liked some of what was sold off the rack, but if I required anything special, such as a party dress, it was made for me by the head dressmaker, Mrs Mounsey. She would come to measure me, and we'd pick a pattern. That was all very well, until it came to the final fitting and all the assistants would come to see what it looked like, with the corresponding 'oohs' and 'aahs'. There was always the opportunity, of course, to get things at cost price and that was another discernible benefit.

When my brother eventually bought his first house, Mother suggested that he take advantage of the Allens' opportunity. I remember her clearly saying Michael was so mean, as he asked if it was better to wait for a sale than buy at cost price. 'Doesn't he realise the cost price is still cheaper than sale price?' she observed.

During my teenage years it was great to live in a seaside town and have the entertainment on hand. As I got older we would go to dances on a Saturday night, and being the 60s, we got some great groups. The Beatles never came to Bridlington, but I did go with a group from the youth club when they appeared in Scarborough and saw them there, or perhaps it was Hull? I do remember it cost ten shillings. The Beatles was the pop group of the day and Oggy remembers us organising a mile of pennies for charity, with one row of pennies for each Beatle. I provided four posters and stuck them to individual boards to head each line of coins. It was a competition, of course, to see which Beatle got the most support. However Miss Heafford confiscated the posters and a donation had to be made to get them back.

As I have already recorded, amusement arcades were out of bounds and I usually never rebelled on that accord. I was brought up strictly, with Granny effectively ruling the roost, and there were certain ways to do things. You could never lick an ice cream, only bite it. But of course that was cold on one's teeth so we had to bite with our lips!

Ice cream was the only food item we were allowed to consume outside at the beach hut.

Then, of course, there was the way to eat, not eat, to speak, or not speak, and so on and so on. It was most difficult and often more than a little confusing.

In Bridlington I was told not to say 'pardon' but rather to say 'what'? But when visiting my father my aunt would tell me not to say 'what' but 'pardon'. The same applied to 'dessert' and 'pudding'. One day I told Granny I was so hot I was sweating. 'Adrienne,' she admonished, 'horses sweat, men perspire and ladies breathe.' Similarly, my grandmother and indeed Mother would look down on people who held their knife the 'wrong' way.

Nor was I allowed to get a holiday job, as most of my friends did. How could any grand-daughter of Mrs Allen be seen working in a café?

I joined the Brownies and enjoyed it. Mother became Brown Owl and her friend Tawny Owl.

The bungalow we lived in was good and there were friends to play with in the road, at the end of which there was a golf course. We would often stray onto it as there was a pond with tadpoles, and later on, of course, frogs. We occasionally annoyed the golfers by stealing their balls. That mischievous activity was usually led by my brother, but he was rarely alone. The steward lived at the end of the road next to the club and if he caught us, there would be trouble. We called him Copper Kettle.

By the golf club were riding stables and we would often go there to try and help out. The stables were run by the eldest Turner girl, who was one of four. Two of her younger sisters were my regular babysitters when Mother went out.

On Guy Fawkes' night we would help build a huge bonfire at the golf club. We went round the houses asking if people had anything for the fire then dragged it through the streets, to the club. Bonfire nights were always fun, except when some particularly nasty boys would try to put jumping crackers down our Wellington boots.

I remember our neighbours in Belvedere Road. Mrs Hicks lived next door. She was a recluse who peeped out from behind her curtains and I'm afraid we did not always speak kindly of her. But when she was ill, Mother was always ready to help. Next door but one lived Mrs Busfield along with her disabled daughter, Pauline, who was paralysed from the neck down and Mother was very good about going to visit, sometimes taking me.

In those days door-to-door milk deliveries were still in operation. Our milk was delivered by an elderly chap and his daughter using a horse and cart. I believe the father must have been about 90. They lived in a derelict farmhouse set in a large field to the back of our bungalow. Again, instigated by my rebel of a brother, we would climb over the back fence into the field and on several occasions we even managed to creep into the farmhouse. I'm not sure why. I suppose it was a childish case of follow the leader.

Mother and I were very happy in the bungalow. We had a Siamese cat, Pixie, whom we adored. But when she caught birds, mice and once a rabbit, it was me who had to rescue the animal and either bury it or set it free. My mother was very squeamish about those things.

Mother and I would go to church on Sunday. We would walk, and always tried to get there early because if we didn't we would run into the boarders from the high school, and they walked so slowly in crocodile form. Church was always non-negotiable, but I did enjoy it, and today I am still traditional in the way I like this type of service to be. At school we always had morning prayers – a 10 to 15 minute service – and then a nice hymn.

After church on Sunday we would then go off to my grandparents for lunch. My grandfather had a sweet tooth and he had a sweetie drawer full of different chocolate bars. Mother and I were allowed to choose one or two bars each to take home. We would then sit and watch the old Sunday television movie at home.

Shopping was a very different experience then as there were no supermarkets. You either went into the grocery shop with your list, read out an item, the grocer got it, put it onto the counter and so on, or you gave the grocer the list and it was delivered later that day by a delivery boy on a bike. We always checked off every single item carefully to make sure everything was there and the price was right. That is something very few people would bother to do today.

In our bungalow the only form of heating was an open fire and it was my job to clean it out and re-lay it every morning, ready to light in the evening. There were heaters in the bedrooms. Mother would wake up first and then come to turn my heater on and wake me.

My aunt and uncle by this time had moved from 14 St James Road to 150 Cardigan Road. It was a very nice detached house with large grounds. My uncle also bought a semi-detached property next door and developed it into two flats. That was a very nice earner and he did not have to look far for buyers. He encouraged his parents, May and Ernest Green, to buy the ground floor flat and he also encouraged my grandparents to buy Mother the top floor flat. It was larger than the bungalow, and very nicely furnished, courtesy of Allens. But we lost our garden, open fields at the back, friends - and Pixie. The road was much busier and one night she was killed by a car. I remember being so sad.

The arrangement at the flat was that we shared the garden with the Greens. That was not the same as being able to walk out of the back door into your own. I also had to keep the music down as the Greens complained at the slightest sound, even footsteps.

~ *Four* ~

Staying on at high school until 18, I was then given the opportunity of going to finishing school in Switzerland. As with the boarding school, my grandparents were to pay. But I really didn't want to go, and going to university was not something I was interested in. I didn't consider myself to be academic and was keen – indeed quite excited – about the prospect of taking my place in the adult workforce.

I really didn't know what I wanted to do career-wise but in my youthful wisdom I decided to go to off to the London College of Secretaries. That choice somewhat reflected my mother's advice when I was younger to do a secretarial course, as it was always something to fall back on in later years if times got tough.

My course was to last nine months and since I was but a country girl keen to experience city life I signed up as a college resident. Although I was nervous about sharing a room with a total stranger, I was lucky enough to be teamed up with someone who was very like me in lots of ways. We got on well, enjoying most weekends in London seeing the normal sights, and doing the usual, independently elder teenage things. It was at times carefree and we had a lot of fun.

While going through college I saw much more of my father, which was wonderful. He had taken to sailing, and I enjoyed it. I would have enjoyed sailing in Bridlington had the opportunity been provided. My uncle and aunt had a yacht and raced most weekends. Mother and I were only invited out on the first day of Regatta Week. Those were the days of the sail-past when the racing effectively started. Each team was judged on the appearance of its yacht and the crew. We wore white slacks and blue and white striped tops. But Mother and I were never invited to take part in any race. I believe my aunt was not keen on me going anyway because she said the language was rather 'blue' at the best of times. But what else could she expect from any macho bunch of eager, hyper, adrenaline-pumped men, competing not only against themselves, but the elements too.

So I would mostly sail with Dad. Michael was not interested in sailing with us, much to my father's disappointment since he often took part in yacht races with my uncle in Bridlington when on leave. My uncle considered Michael to be a very useful member of his racing team, so he was often invited.

During my teenage years I jokingly maintained my mother was never going to get a new husband until I left home. I was right. She married Bill Hopps within four months of me going to college. Mother was 41 then and Bill was about 35. He was a fabulous chap, such fun and a great laugh.

Bill had a twin brother, Tony, and they both joined the Midland Bank workforce when they left school. Bill didn't progress, staying with the Bridlington Branch until he retired, always as a cashier. He really didn't want to move up the ranks, indicating he hated every minute in the bank. I often thought it was such a shame to spend your life doing a job you hated. Unlike his twin, Tony went on to much bigger and better things, being transferred to the Guernsey branch as manager at one time.

Bill and Tony were Masons and Mother's new husband managed to persuade us that the members of that organisation were not just a load of old cranks who held secret meetings, but that they actually did some good in the world. He was also a member of the Masons' offshoot, the Knights Templar, and we had many drunken nights with him getting into all his regalia and brandishing his sword.

Bill and Mother married on Christmas Eve 1966. It was a register office wedding with a small reception at Aunty Ruth's house. Sally, Madeleine and I were there, and it was for the most part a family affair except for some of Bill's best friends. Michael didn't come to Mother's wedding. He was posted in a not so distant country – Germany. He probably didn't have leave.

I believe this was the first time I had too much to drink, as did Sally. I was 18 at that time. Sally was 16 and a very pretty attractive girl. We were good friends. I was to have spent that night at Aunty Ruth's; but she was not happy with either of us. We were both violently ill and well and truly in disgrace.

However one of the younger wedding guests, the son of Bill's best friend, called round later and asked if we wanted to go with him to the rugby club. I agreed to go but Sally was not allowed to. Aunty Ruth would have liked to have stopped me too, but she couldn't as I was 18. She seemed to have conveniently forgotten for a moment the fun she had and the trouble she caused as a youngster!

Bill and Mother moved from the flat in Cardigan Road to a semi-detached house in St James Road which they had bought through a cheap mortgage with his bank. Bill did not want to be beholden to my grandparents for accommodation and quite rightly so. I remember Mother saying later she was put out by the fact that she didn't get all of the proceeds of the sale of the flat – they were divided between her, Ruth, and, I think, Judith as Richard's widow.

Mother settled well into her married life. I decided to stay in London after the nine month college course to get a job. A residential college friend, Jane, and I first thought about going to Bournemouth as she rather liked it there, but I wasn't sure. I really wanted to stay in London and our teachers told us we would be foolish not to get experience in London first. So we stayed, and I shared a flat with another residential college friend, Sue, and two of the day girls. Our first flat was in West Cromwell Road, Earls Court. It consisted of a sitting room, kitchen, bathroom and one bedroom. With the four of us sharing we paid £14 a week between us. Coincidentally, my first salary was also £14 a week.

I initially went to work for a firm of solicitors in the city and gained excellent experience there. However, I was specialising in divorce cases, which became rather depressing especially when I had to witness parents fighting over custody of the children. That brought back too many bad memories for me.

I keenly remember moving into that first flat with my friends, with the observation from another friend that while we thought we were friends then, we may have a different view in six months. We couldn't believe there would be any problems, but of course there were and at the end of six months, Sue had had enough and said she was leaving. So then there were three.

We got another flat in Maida Vale and a memorable moment was created there. One day a film crew knocked on our door, asking if they could shoot about 30 seconds for a short scene from The Avengers. Of course we said yes as we to be were paid a minimal amount. But we were unable to use the front door for the period they were filming and the 30 seconds, of course, lasted about two hours!

The scene consisted of someone running up, knocking on the door and then entering. We watched from the window, but to our horror, we spotted Bill and my mother walking towards our flat. They were in London to visit me and were staying at a local hotel.

I could just picture them breezing up, my mother making small talk with the producers and managing to get into the shoot, but it turned out okay.

But the old adage that two is company and three is a crowd was alive and well and I was the next to feel pushed out of sharing. It was by then summer however and I felt it was time to take a long break as I was missing those long school holidays.

As well as spending time in Bridlington I had a memorable sailing trip with Dad which involved crossing the Channel to Cherbourg in France. I had complete trust in him as sailor and navigator, but I think it was rather by good luck than management that we actually arrived at our destination. We ran into a thunderstorm close to France. There was lightning, heavy rain, the sea got wild, and there was a confusing array of lights. As a result, my father was uncertain of where the harbour entrance was. After such a good clear run, it was a disappointment to us since we expected to be in the Cherbourg Yacht Club that night. But as it was, we sailed up the coast until dawn, and then came back in the morning to the harbour.

We made several acquaintances in Cherbourg, including the crew of a big launch we were to meet again. We hired a car ashore - which cost Dad more than the rest of the holiday - then we drove down to Mont St Michel and St Malo.

Our land-based excursion over, we left Cherbourg and crept along the coast before finding the lovely little harbour of Omanville. We had used a library book guide to get us there and stayed overnight.

The next day, we sailed for Alderney. Dad had some trouble with the Seagull engine, which would slowly lose power. Being cautious, he had had it overhauled before this sailing, but off Cap de la Hague the wind failed and we needed the engine to counter the very strong current. Suddenly the Seagull failed, with not another boat in sight for quite some time. But Dad's red shirt miraculously caught the attention of a passing launch and they offered to tow us to Jersey. We hadn't intended going that far, but there would be good engine overhaul facilities there, so it was agreed. Once in Jersey the engine was handed over to the local Seagull agent.

The big launch Pipella we had met in Cherbourg joined us in the yacht basin with a middle-aged couple aboard. Our engine repaired, we then got ready to sail for Guernsey and this couple pointed out that we were going to 'buck the tide'.

Dad admitted he knew this, but said if we could get a little way out it would help when the tide turned. The couple on Pipella advised us we should not leave then, but when Dad ignored them, they said they would keep a watchful eye out for us. With their twin diesels they would have no trouble setting to sea against the incoming tide.

Getting away from Jersey was slow going, and early in the afternoon we hove to and brewed a cup of tea. After sailing again, we cleared Corbière. The sea was calm, there was little wind and it was a beautiful afternoon.

Dad said he would run the engine for an hour or so and just then I observed Pipella, altering course toward us. They were a mile off, but steered to come alongside.

The couple were amused, telling Dad he should have taken their advice and offering to tow us to Guernsey, where we could all have a night ashore together. I supported this idea, and with three against one, Dad agreed and off we went. It was a lovely evening under a clear, turquoise blue sky.

We were six miles off Sark and I was rather shocked on realising Pipella's engines had stopped. Thirty or forty yards astern in the water I saw the lady from that craft. Dad shouted, asking if she could swim, but when it became obvious she couldn't – she was struggling to keep her head above water - he dived over the side and swam to her. She was very good and showed no real panic. Dad turned her on her back and they started back toward Pipella. Later he told me from the water the launch looked like the side of a house, with quite a climb to the deck. But with an almighty and somewhat un-gentlemanly heave from where he could get the most leverage, he got her up onto the boarding ladder.

Fortunately, we were experiencing a slack tide otherwise we might have been in real trouble. That night we had dinner aboard Pipella. They had literally everything on board, a refrigerator, an oven and the equipment required for life on the ocean waves. We had a beautiful three-course meal, and wine of course. The latter provided the fortitude to allow us to ask the burning question – what had happened? The launch lady was adamant that she did not know. She observed there had been hardly a ripple, that she was up in the cockpit, not on the fore-deck, and she just could not give any explanation as to how she got in the water. For me it was an amazing thing to see a life being saved, more so that it was my own father who undertook the rescue mission. I was so proud of him.

Upon leaving Guernsey, our next intended port of call was Alderney, the most northerly of the Channel islands and the one closest to both

France and the United Kingdom. We had this long thin island well in our sights but the wind was gusting almost to gale force and we knew we were in trouble. However, still having complete trust in Dad I really do not remember being worried. But it was night before we made it into the harbour, and Dad and I knew we still had a long beat to make the jetty. He was exhausted and he knew I didn't have the strength to take over, so he made a decision to let off a flare.

His theory was that people ashore would have been watching us, and thinking we were safely in the harbour they most likely would relax and go to bed. So off went the flare, and within a short time a fishing boat loomed up in the darkness with two men aboard. One leapt onto our deck and with a line aboard and sails down, they pulled us the fair distance to the jetty.

We were wet, extremely tired, and very hungry and the hunger pains, coupled with our gale-induced exhaustion, were overpowering. Leaving our yacht at the jetty, we marched up to the only pub to see if dinner was still being served. It wasn't, but the barman took great pity on us, realising we formed the entire crew of the near-stricken yacht. He suggested they would do dinner if we wouldn't mind eating in the kitchen and, of course, we didn't. It was a marvellous meal.

But our adventures were far from over as we still had to get back to England and Alderney is 60 miles from the south coast of the United Kingdom mainland. We set off in rather calm seas, but then the fog came down. We knew we were in the middle of one of the world's busiest shipping lanes, the English Channel, literally going nowhere fast, with dense fog all around. Then we heard an outboard motor approaching and out of the mist an inflatable dinghy appeared with two men aboard. They were clearly horrified when they saw us, but as soon as we indicated we were okay, they sped off.

Two or three minutes later, they returned, clearly worried about us since they were unable to tow us. They reckoned we would be at sea all night, but they left once more, after we agreed to phone them when we eventually got in.

Once again, good luck was on our side and we made it to England, albeit the next day. The thought of it now horrifies me since it could have been a very different outcome, but I always had faith in my father.

Summer over, and still being friendly with some of the girls from college, I decided to share with Jane and Ruth and one of her school friends, Helen. We got a flat in Belsize Park with two bedrooms this time, one being a single. Helen was happy to take the single and the rest of us shared the double.

I secured another job for a lock and safe company but although it was not terribly interesting, I stuck it out for a year.

Occasionally I went down to Brighton and obtained permission to take Sally out from Roedean for the day. She was thrilled to be able to escape and we always had a lot of fun.

~ *Five* ~

When Michael got leave, he would spend a lot of time in London and usually slept on the floor of our flat. There was always space for him as far as I was concerned and he got on well with my flat mates. He particularly liked Ruth, but her heart was elsewhere.

Michael and I got on extremely well during these times. We wrote to each other, phoned and even went on holiday together once. He had met a lovely Dutch family while in Germany and he took me to visit them. We had a great time. He also introduced me to Amsterdam.

After three years in London I began to get itchy feet. Any thought of me going to Bournemouth with Jane had disappeared. She was happy living in London and I wanted to go abroad. At the time there were still £10 deals for migration to Australia. The prospect was very appealing but the rules required that one had to stay in Australia a minimum of two years and, at the age of 21, that sounded a long time if you didn't like it. South Africa had a similar scheme. It would cost £30, but there were no minimum time requirements. I was told 'if you do not like our country Madam you are able to leave the next day.'

I tried my best to persuade someone to come with me. Jane? Ruth? Helen? In each case it was a no. Sue was still a good friend, but was now married and I'd talk to her and her husband John about it. One day John said to me 'For heaven's sake Adrienne, stop talking about South Africa. You will never go.'

To this day if someone tells me I can't do something it makes me even more determined. So I made arrangements to go to South Africa alone, with my departure set for the 14th November 1969.

Before that however I decided I wanted to spend a bit of time on the Continent and I managed to persuade Helen to come with me. Au pairs were all the thing in France and we were told we could just go out, meet up with an agency and be placed then and there with a family. Of course we found out it wasn't quite as easy as it sounded. Helen and I got to Marseilles, where Helen was offered a place with a single mother and her young son. My job offer was in a small nearby village called Cassis. We really wanted to be closer to each other but with choices few and far between, we took up our respective jobs.

Cassis was delightful and I just loved it there, but I did not enjoy the family. As it turned out the husband was English and his wife was French, and they ran a restaurant. Their daughter was 15 and hardly in need of an au pair, while their son was aged 10. Even at that age the boy really did what he wanted.

My engagement as an au pair was not what I expected – the wife simply wanted me to wash and clean, particularly for the restaurant. Each day I started with the breakfast dishes. This was not onerous you would have thought, but oh my, how very particular this woman was. I can wash dishes and was often required to do so, but she insisted not one iota of soap suds must be left on the item before you dried it in the days before dishwashers. Okay, rinse, rinse, rinse; but have you tried to rinse a sieve to get all the soap suds out – very difficult. And a lot of the time she would just stand there watching me because she didn't go to the restaurant until about midday. Then there was laundry for the restaurant – not by any stretch of an imagination au pair work - table cloths, napkins and the like. But they too had to be just so perfect.

Of course the idea of going as au pair to another country is to learn the language. Here was I, a failure at French A level. But I did learn one awful lot of swear words from the wife, with most of them directed at me unfortunately. The daughter was not very nice to me either, but she was very pretty and liked the boys. I felt she was against me because one boy in particular spent rather more time with me than with her. As a consequence she told childish tales about me to her mother, which made matters worse.

There was however an escape mechanism, having every afternoon and evening off. Cassis was such a lovely place and I met a group of English people, about six of them, boys and girls, and I'd join them on their outings.

One day we all went to Marseilles and looked up Helen in the apartment where she was staying. She was not having a good time either, with her employer also being a very strict French lady. So strict was she that poor Helen was petrified when we all turned up on the doorstep. Helen did ask us in, but she was concerned that the young boy she was caring for would tell his mother she had friends around.

After their two week holiday I learned my English friends were heading for home by car. One of the boys, Chris, knew it was not really working out for me and as he had his own car he said I could return with him, while the others shared the other vehicles. I agreed and Helen decided she was coming home too. In those days I was quite a nervous girl and I was frightened by the thought of having to tell my French boss I was leaving. I packed my bag one afternoon and left it tucked under the bed, but lo-and-behold when I returned later that day the wife said she had found my bag and demanded to know why I was packed and ready to go. I was of course upset she had gone through my room, and this showed me what type of woman she was, so that was it – off I went. It took a couple of days to get home and we camped out one night en route back to the United Kingdom. It was such fun.

I was destined to go to South Africa however and my father and a friend took me to Southampton to see me off on the liner Edinburgh Castle. I had decided to sail rather than fly because I thought it would give me the opportunity to meet people, which it did. It was a dull murky day when I left Southampton and my father described how he watched me sail into the rain, standing at the rail and visible for a long time in my bright green coat!

During the two weeks I was on that voyage I met with many others who were migrating and some of the officers, striking up a real friendship with Bob.

It was a good trip and I crossed the international dateline for the first time. The crew held a King Neptune ceremony, which was traditional at such times, and they ended up throwing cream cakes and dunking people in the pool. The rest of the voyage was spent with the usual activities, not unlike those on cruises these days, but obviously not quite so sophisticated. I vividly remember the glorious food.

We arrived in Cape Town early one morning and I recall getting up especially early that day to see our approach. My first sight of Table Mountain appearing was one I shall never forget.

We migrants were soon bedded in hotel accommodation, with our expenses being paid until we got a job. I arrived in early December and quite quickly got a job with an insurance company, beginning in the New Year. That was great, the Christmas break, with all expenses being covered under the immigration scheme.

At that time the Union Castle Line ships came out from England to South Africa every week. Their first port of call was Cape Town and they would then go up the coast to Port Elizabeth and Durban, before returning to Cape Town, which was great. Then it was the return voyage, to the United Kingdom, and so on and so on.

The week after the 'Eddy' came out, the SA Vaal arrived. More people
– usually girls – were booked into my hotel, and I met Peggy and Sheila.
They were to become lifelong friends. Peggy was a nurse and Sheila a
secretary. Peggy secured a job at Groote Schuur Hospital and decided to
live in as accommodation was cheap and good. So Sheila and I decided
to share, renting a bed-sit in Upper Orange Street.

The bed-sit had a communal bathroom and we seemed to manage
with our little cooking facilities, which mostly consisted of one electric
fry pan. There were two other rooms to rent in the house. One was a
single taken by a girl called Penny. The other was rented by two young
men, Barry and Tony who became good friends too. On her days off
Peggy would come and stay. The place was so small she had to sleep on a
mattress under the table!

Sheila had also struck up a friendship with an officer on the Vaal,
so we would get invited to their parties on board when he was in port.
Another friend, Janet, arrived aboard the Windsor Castle and she was
such a laugh and good fun. Once a week those ships would arrive and
whereas it is often said sailors have a girl in every port, there is a flip side
of the coin. Some girls had a sailor on every ship! We knew a lot of nurses
and the officers would phone the hospitals to ask them to parties and
we'd get the word too. These were indeed fun times.

I enjoyed life in Cape Town. The city was so beautiful and the weather
was good. We'd walk to work every day through the park. I spent my first
hot Christmas on the beach with friends. That was very different to my
home country, but something I was definitely going to get used to. We
toured around a lot, as there was no television in South Africa in those
days. That seemed strange to begin with but we quickly got used to it
and in the end we made our own fun. I experienced my first earthquake
in Cape Town, much to my surprise. I didn't realise such natural events
happened in that country. When the shaking started we were so startled.
I remember asking Penny if she realised it was an earthquake? She hadn't
and made the comment she thought it was 'you lot making the usual
noise'. She was the quiet one in our house

Winter was about to arrive in Cape Town and Peggy, Sheila and I
decided to head for Durban where we knew it would be warmer. Tony
decided to come too, and we expected Barry would join him, but
surprisingly he did not. The reason emerged later, as unbeknown to us,
Barry had struck up a close relationship with our quiet little Penny and
had a reason for staying behind. I think they got married eventually.

Peggy, Sheila and I travelled up to Durban on the Vaal. Bob had been 'laid off' from the 'Eddy' and was not on that ship any more. Tony went up under his own steam. We had remained friendly with Janet and she joined us in Durban.

Durban was lovely but accommodation was hard to find. The only place within our price range was 36 Delrenee Mansions. We could never forget the address. The trouble with Durban was it was a popular holiday destination in the winter because it was much warmer than the Cape. But the popularity caused the prices to soar and my first sight of No. 36 was one of horror. The place was riddled with cockroaches. At first I said resolutely I would not live there, but we just could not find anything else reasonable and Sheila persuaded me, insisting we could clean it up, which we did.

There were two big rooms which we decided to turn into two bed-sitting rooms. Peggy and Janet slept in one and Sheila and I in the other. We settled well into Durban life although I had felt guilty about giving my notice in at my work in Cape Town. When I first secured the job, my boss had observed I would soon be off to Durban for the winter, but I'd promised him that would not happen. He was such a nice man, but he was right, I did want to go to Durban. I then made up all sorts of tales about having to go back to the United Kingdom, which did not sit well with me, and later I swore I would never put myself in such a position again.

In Durban I opted to do temporary work and that worked out well because I ended up being with one company, Roberts Construction, the whole time I was living in that city. The people I met in Durban were such fun. Among them was Jan, who will always be remembered for his Snoopy the Red Baron impressions around our flat with one of our bras on his head as an airman's helmet, and Paddy and Bill, the Irish lads. We had a great circle of friends. I had no particular boyfriend during this time, being part of a really good group of friends. Tony was one of them, and I know he really liked me, but he was just a special friend who would always be there for me.

On Friday nights we would all frequent the pub across the road, which had a resident folk singer. At the end of the night everyone would sing the popular folk ballad 'The Leaving of Liverpool' which still reminds me of those days.

Apart from our pub nights and wide range of activities in and around Durban, we travelled a lot too, even managing one trip to Mozambique.

Durban was good for the winter but got very hot in the summer. So Sheila, Peggy and I followed the trend and went to Johannesburg to earn more money. It was no surprise to me that Tony came too! He met up with a mate who had a flat and stayed with him. We girls would never have let him share with us because although he was my special friend, we reckoned he cramped our style!

When we left Durban a great group was there, on the train platform, to see us off. On arrival at Jo-burg, we booked into the annex of the Rondebosch Hotel and immediately enjoyed the luxury of our very own bathroom and kitchenette.

During our first day in Johannesburg, Sheila, Peggy and I went for a walk to have a look around. Down the road came this white Alpha Romeo with two gorgeous young men in it. I decided to give them a wave and a 'hello', whereupon the Alpha came to a screeching halt and Raf and Elio entered our lives. They were Italian, or in Raf's case, one should say Sicilian.

Elio became my on-off boyfriend, although he once said to me he would never marry me. That did not perturb me as I had no intention of marrying him. I knew he had another girlfriend and at that time I would basically go out with anyone who asked.

While in Johannesburg, I took another temping job, with a pharmaceutical company. Through that company I met a couple of English lads and we got into their social circle, as well as the great crowd living at the Rondebosch.

Our rent at that hotel included breakfast and each morning we would go into the dining room. We always had the same waiter and we would always order exactly the same breakfast – for me a boiled egg. Our waiter knew this and, trying to be helpful, always had the egg ready and waiting. The trouble was it had probably been there for about half an hour, and by the time I came to eat it, it was hard boiled and cold.

One day Elio had to work late and even though we had a date he decided to take one of the coloured workers home, as this man had missed his bus. This man lived in Soweto and it was an interesting experience driving there, but not one I would probably repeat now. We survived the experience without trouble, but it was a prolonged outing as we drove around and around, because this coloured man couldn't remember where he lived. To me all the shacks looked the same, especially in the dark, and all the Soweto streets were so very similar. At that time South Africa was entrenched in the apartheid era, and coloured people were not allowed to travel on buses with Whites, eat in the same restaurants or sit on the same beaches.

One of the trips Sheila, Peggy and I enjoyed was to Kruger National Park, which was, even then, highly valued as a wildlife sanctuary. We did this trip on the cheap and by ourselves, without the benefit of being on a guided tour, with all the luxuries, as is the case these days.

As a photographic expedition, this trip was something of a disaster. All of my photos consisted of blurry shots of animals some distance off! But it was quite an experience. Sheila and I also went to Rhodesia, as it was called in those days. Now it is Zimbabwe.

We went with three young men. Eggy was one of them – an appropriate nickname for someone with a bald head.

While in Rhodesia, we visited Salisbury and the Zimbabwe Ruins, before travelling into Zambia to see the Kariba Dam and Victoria Falls. It was another of our memorable trips, of which we seemed to be blessed with many.

I always knew Sheila had New Zealand in her sights as an eventual destination so we decided to set off, via Australia, with Peggy. However the trip was almost booked when Peggy dropped a bombshell – she would not be coming with us. She was going to stay in Johannesburg with Raf, and so she did. They married and are still there to this day, having two boys, who now live in Italy.

To our surprise, and to my personal horror, Tony announced he was coming to Australia too. I knew he liked me a lot, but I was uncomfortable with the thought of having him following me all around the world. I knew there would never be anything in it as far as I was concerned, but obviously Tony had not received my messages.

To avoid confronting what was fast becoming an issue for me, Sheila and I hatched a plan which I now consider to be one of the most horrible things I have done at any time in my life. We told Tony we were booked for Australia on one ship, but then travelled on another. We never saw him again, but it was an example of me being much too frightened to tell people exactly what I thought or wanted. I never wanted to hurt people and I certainly didn't want to hurt Tony, so I do hope things turned out well for him and he ended up being really happy.

~ *Six* ~

We spent just fourteen months in South Africa, but we welcomed the prospect of a trip 'Down Under'. We sailed from Durban to Perth, on the western coast of Australia, meeting a good crowd. I befriended a couple of Swiss lads who were heading to New Zealand and grew very fond of Jacky, spending a lot of time with him.

Our travelling companion to Zimbabwe, Eggy, had returned to his home city of Perth and met the ship when it arrived. He spent the entire day driving us around the sights in Perth. We must have travelled 200 miles that day. The ship then sailed for Melbourne, where we bumped into someone we knew from Durban, proof indeed that it was certainly a small world. After Melbourne we sailed to Sydney, the final destination of this part of our trip to this far-flung outreach of the former British Empire.

In Sydney, Sheila and I decided we would answer an advertisement seeking two girls to share a house and we went to view it in Rose Bay. It was very nice, but it did not have a bath. I had never lived in a house without a bath, and I didn't want to, although the two girls, Robyn and Leah, were very nice. But once again Sheila talked me round and we moved in.

Both our house-mates were Australian. Leah had a boyfriend who was an officer on one of the ships, which seemed to be common ground there, and Robyn was just lovely, a true friend to this day.

Again I opted for temporary work, working for P&O the whole time I lived in Sydney. Sheila worked for a travel agent. It proved to be very useful having such employers. We settled into Australian life, trying to see as much as we could. I was corresponding with Jacky who had by now arrived in New Zealand.

I had gone to South Africa with just £100 in my pocket, then worked, spent, saved and travelled, so we never had enough money for a car. I lived literally hand to mouth, so we took up hitch-hiking, which worked well.

We also joined the Youth Hostel Association so we could avail ourselves of cheap accommodation. The hostels did tend to be well off the beaten track and were usually sparse, so much of the time we were the only people staying. We certainly had to take everything we needed and the toilet – the dunny as the Australians so eloquently called it - was usually an open hole in the ground. In one of the 'facilities', the notes warned to beware as there was often a snake in the dunny. My visits there were very short!

During one hitch-hiking expedition we met Gabriel, a Brazilian. We became friendly and he took a real shine to me. He did not like us hitch-hiking, warning us that not everyone was as nice as he was. When we told Gabriel we were planning to hitch-hike from Sydney to Adelaide, then up to Ayers Rock, across to Cairns, and then down the coast, he was quite horrified and said he would take us in his little Volkswagen.

Gabriel was simply marvellous to us. We camped a lot of the time, especially up through the Red Centre and he is another person I feel guilty about because, in hindsight, I do not feel I treated him very well.

While in Adelaide I looked up an old school friend of Mother's called Rosemary and she invited Sheila, Gabriel and I to dinner. Her lovely husband was there also. Then we really got stuck into the Outback – miles and miles of nothing but red dust which got everywhere, even though we had taken care to wrap everything up in polythene.

Half way to the opal mining town Coober Pedy, we came across a car which had broken down. We stopped to see if we could help, even though we couldn't really. The man who seemed to be in charge was Arabic, or was at least Arab-looking, and went by the name of Farid. He was very pleasant and thanked us for stopping, but said they would be fine.

Coober Pedy was an amazing place. It had an all-male population and we soon observed that Sheila and I appeared to be the only two girls there. In the pub we saw Farid and his crew and we soon discovered he was quite a 'big man' in that community. Farid bought us dinner and drinks all night, which went down really well and gave us confidence that we had done the right thing by stopping to offer assistance earlier. Good karma as they say.

In Coober Pedy one feature of the landscape that amazed us was the underground caves where people lived to escape the incredible heat experienced in that region of the Outback.

We then travelled north, to Alice Springs and Ayers Rock, which is now known as Uluru. They don't like you climbing it now, but in those days many people did so and Sheila, Gabriel and I were among them. We literally had to pull ourselves up by a chain initially. It was a tough walk, but I am glad I did it.

We decided not to try and make it to Darwin, instead crossing from Tennant Creek to the east coast and exiting the desert at Townsville. I remember taking a boat trip out to the Whitsunday Islands and thinking at that time it was the best day of my life. It was so beautiful in that part of coastal North Queensland, with its tropical rainforests and the stunning Great Barrier Reef.

On this trip we were away about three weeks and it was tough going with just the three of us travelling together and in such close confines for long distances in that little Volkswagen. We had a few disagreements with Gabriel and when that occurred, he would sulk for a while, but I remained friendly with him. Gabriel was a photographer and took a lot of beautiful photos of me, and the scenery, some of which I still have. After I left Australia, I continued writing to him for a while but the correspondence soon fizzled out.

Overall we stayed in Sydney for about five months, just long enough to plan the most amazing trip home to the United Kingdom, via New Zealand. Working in the travel agency, Sheila was able to get very good deals and as I was with P&O I booked a berth from Nassau in the Bahamas to Southampton in England. It is not usual to be able to book a voyage out of a country, with the traditional path being 'in' and then 'out' again, but we were not sure at that time how we wanted to get to Nassau so we wanted to leave it open.

The first leg of the trip was to Auckland and on arrival we secured a small house in Herne Bay. We thought we were really going up in the world, with a separate lounge, bedroom, bathroom and kitchen – even though there were rats running around inside the walls. Sheila and I both got jobs at the Waitemata City Council, albeit it in different departments.

Leah had given us the name of her friend in Auckland, Mike, who introduced us to his crowd, so we settled in well. These were the days of six o'clock closing of the pubs and hence they had what was known as the six o'clock swill. Just before closing time everyone would charge across the road straight from work to the Carpenters Arms and drink as much as quickly as they could, swilling it down like there was no tomorrow.

During one of those 'swill sessions' we met Ian, who also worked for the council. After the pub closed Ian asked Sheila and I to have dinner with him at his favourite haunt, the Troika. During what was a beautiful dinner – Ian was obviously well known at this restaurant – I quietly informed Sheila I reckoned he fancied her. But the next day – my birthday – I received a very nice green stone bracelet, leaving Sheila amused and concluding it was me Ian really fancied.

At that time I was, however, seeing Jacky, the Swiss chap, although it was somewhat on and off. We went off for a few weekends together and in particular I paid my first visit to the Tongariro National Park in the centre of the North Island.

Jacky and his friend Rolf were ski instructors and we stayed at one of the chalets on the Ruapehu ski-field. That was my first and last time on skis, as the boys went off to do their own thing instead of giving me their expert tuition in the appalling weather.

Ian's father owned a boat and Ian took us all around the Hauraki Gulf, stopping in the little bays of the beautiful islands just out from Auckland. It was wonderful. We also sailed right up to the Bay of Islands one Christmas and had a couple of weeks exploring that area.

I developed a good friendship with a girl called Jacqui, who was always a barrel of laughs and she and I would go off together at weekends on occasions. On one of these expeditions we were unable to find anywhere to stay at one isolated beach, so we ended up sleeping under an upturned rowing boat.

Sheila and I hitch-hiked our way around South Island - right down to Invercargill - and thoroughly enjoyed it. Once when we were languishing on a roadside, waiting for a non-existent lift, we got talking to a man out walking. He asked where we came from, and when I said 'Bridlington', he insisted we accompany him to his house, to meet his wife. She had come from Bridlington and of course she knew Allens. Everyone from Bridlington knew of Allens! As the story of Bridlington unfolded, I found that this woman used to work for Carltons, Allens' biggest rival, so that was a very interesting meeting. Later this couple gave us a ride to a far better spot where we were more likely to get picked up.

We also visited Christchurch, where my father had cousins. Although he never kept in touch, my Aunt Marjorie wrote to all the cousins so we were encouraged to look them up. The two cousins there were Valerie and Shirley and their mother was my grandmother's sister. Valerie was married to Arnold and they treated us very well, although it was quite an experience. We stayed with them and met Shirley and her family. Valerie seemed to live in a time warp. Their house, I think, had remained unchanged for many years and still had an outside toilet.

Another of my hitch-hiking expeditions with Jacqui proved extremely interesting, to say the least. We decided to go to The Grand Château, the majestic old hotel on the slopes of Mount Ruapehu, in the Tongariro National Park. We managed to get a fair way, but lifts soon became few and far between. Then a run-down old car stopped with an odd looking man inside. Our instincts told us not to take a chance with him, but it was late and we considered we would be two against his one if anything untoward was to occur.

As it developed, we should have stuck with our instincts, staying on the outside of the car, rather than being trapped within it. After some time, the driver veered off the main road and drove for quite a way up a track. I was in the back and Jacqui in the front and in support of each other we demanded to know where he was taking us.

This strange man insisted the track was a short-cut to The Grand Château, but we were not that naïve. Stopping the car some way up the track he declared he would not drive us back until we had sex with him. I reacted as badly as I could, yelling and shouting. The man kept insisting that we give him what he wanted, and then we would all be on our way.

In complete contrast to my agitated approach, Jacqui was absolutely amazing in keeping calm and she signalled to me to be quiet so she could talk. Calmly she suggested that if it was sex he wanted, why didn't he just say so earlier? Her suggestion was that it would be much better in the comfort of a double bed, and we could certainly have a threesome!

With that, we were back up the track again, in the direction we had come from. He drove us back to the main road then to a small town where there was a hotel with accommodation available.

Jacqui suggested a drink first, to which this odd man surprisingly agreed and off we went to the bar. I would have been quite happy to forget the whole thing, have our drink, then stay put, knowing we had others there as witnesses. Jacqui, of course, had other ideas and on opening the door to the pub she stood there yelling 'rapist' at the top of her voice.

The man took to his heels and all hell let loose as the male patrons gave chase. The Police were called and took our statements, with Jacqui calmly telling them the registration number of his car.

A short time later, the Police nabbed the man, who was known to them, and we had to take part in an identity parade. It was not a Police station line-up, but one conducted rural New Zealand style – in the bar packed with local men. The Police placed the guy in the bar, then took

Jacqui and I in separately to point him out. It wasn't difficult at all – everyone in the bar was yelling most derogatory comments and making it very clear where he was positioned. I didn't need help in picking him out, neither did Jacqui, although being the kindly soul that I am, I was concerned that a lynching was on the cards there and then.

We heard later that this man had the book thrown at him. Apart from actually being sent to jail, his driving licence was taken away, he was fined, banned from drinking anywhere, and not allowed to enter any licensed premises for some years. Justice had been done, it seems.

One of the other strange experiences we had in New Zealand occurred in our flat in Auckland. Sheila and I had been out for the night and we gave Jacqui a key so she could stay over. When we arrived home we found the place in a real state, with one window broken, our possessions strewn all around the place, and jewellery out over the sideboard. Having arrived while we were out, Jacqui had gone to bed, but we woke her to ask what happened.

Her explanation was that she thought it was usual – us just being untidy! We had few real valuables at that time and nothing was taken. Some days later we found out why.

I was home alone when there was a knock on the door. A rather large Maori man in white gumboots stood before me, with a large dog. Still naïve - and still too trusting - I asked him what he wanted. His response was that he had been in our flat the other night, and left something behind which he now wanted. Great, a friendly robber! It appears he was disturbed attempting to rob us and thinking he was going to be caught in the act he threw his driver's licence onto the top of the wardrobe. He asked for it back and really not sure how to handle the situation, I gave it to him and after asking me to join him for a drink which I politely declined, off he went, quite happily it seems.

Seven

Our trip home to the United Kingdom was always intended to be a great adventure and it was. Our plan was to sail first to Panama, then travel overland up through Central America, onward to the west coast of America, across Canada, down the east coast to Florida, across to Nassau, and by ship again, to Southampton.

We got a great send off from Auckland, with many of our recently-acquired friends coming to shout and wave, till we disappeared into the Hauraki Gulf and the Pacific Ocean beyond. I for one was disappointed to be leaving behind the great adventures on tap in New Zealand, but at the same time was excited by an entirely new adventure that lay ahead.

On arrival in Panama, the immigration officers came on to the ship to grant us our visas. But all the passengers seemed to be given different time limits for their visits. One was proud to announce they got a month, while another only a week. Sheila got a month, but when I was handed my visa, I found it was for only 48 hours. To say I was highly annoyed is an under-statement. But in reality 48 hours in Panama was more than enough. After our previous experiences, Panama did little for me as a destination, with nothing really exciting to see or do. Sheila felt the same and we crossed the border from Panama into Costa Rica.

The Costa Rican officials went through absolutely everything, looking for drugs. We spent five hours at the border. One Canadian couple was very distraught as the border patrol examined the girl's contraceptive pills, asking poker-faced what they were. The Costa Ricans doing the examining didn't speak English and the Canadians didn't speak Spanish. As the girl had been in Australia, she had in her possession a stuffed koala and she became quite upset when Immigration wanted to cut it open looking for drugs. This couple decided they were not going to tolerate this treatment at every border and opted to fly home. They were going to dump a lot of their possessions as they would have been over their weight limit and naïvely we offered to take one of their bags all the way to Canada as we would be going through their home city of Winnipeg. We did check through the bag to make sure it did not contain drugs or contraband, otherwise we would have been in serious trouble.

After Costa Rica we joined the Tiki bus, travelling up through Central America, Nicaragua, El Salvador, British Honduras, Guatemala and then into Mexico. It certainly was an experience and some of the people we met made the trip intriguing. One was Fred, who was obviously very popular, especially when the bus drove into the depots. He was instantly surrounded by numerous cheerful young people who seemed pleased to see him. Then we realised why - he was a drug trafficker.

Mexico was lovely once we got out of the city centre although before we left to see more of the country we met a couple of men while having dinner. We were at the same table and when we got our separate bills I told them as something of a joke, that our bill was really their bill. Amazingly they took our bill and paid it, then offered to show us around the next day. Unfortunately, we were off to Acapulco on the bus, but the offer was generous, as was the act of paying our restaurant account.

We caught the bus to Acapulco which was a pretty big city even then and it did not have a lot going for it apart from beautiful hotels. Quite cheekily, we would take to just wandering in to the grounds of one of the big hotels, such as the Hilton, and would sit by the pool or have a swim, before heading back to our own accommodation, which of course was a lot less salubrious.

In America we travelled right up the west coast, through Los Angeles, where we visited Disneyland, and then to San Francisco. I was not impressed with the large cities of America, finding them impersonal and unfriendly. In one of those cities I asked a policeman how to get somewhere and was curtly told to buy a map. On a bus, we asked politely if we could go to some particular place, as we often did in the United Kingdom, with the rude response being that we could go where we wanted. I remember that in the smaller cities we fared much better though, the people were friendlier and had a personal touch.

Crossing the border into Canada, we visited Vancouver. We stayed with friends of Sheila's and they showed us around that most beautiful city, before crossing the vast expanse of Canada to Winnipeg to drop off 'that bag.' The reward was a beautiful meal, provided by the young couple who appreciated that we had kept their possessions safe, throughout weeks of travelling from Costa Rica. From Winnipeg we continued on to Montreal where my old friend, Sue and her husband, John, were living. We stayed there for a while and again it was lovely see familiar faces and to be entertained.

We then re-entered the United States, crossing the international border between the Canadian province of Ontario and the American state of New York, with a visit to the stunning triple falls of Niagara en route. Again, we were to be greeted by vast, unfriendly cities – New York and Washington DC – and the fact that it rained for our entire visit didn't endear me to the former one little bit. But we did manage to see Jesus Christ Superstar on Broadway, a highlight if ever there was one.

In Washington, we were dining out and met up with a man who told us he was a policeman. As if to prove it he showed us his gun, although no badge was produced. We just wanted dinner and after eating our meal retired as quickly as possible to our room. But we had only been there for a short time when there was a knock at the door. It was the so-called policeman who wanted to come in. Holding our breath and thinking of the gun, we kept really quiet behind the firmly-closed door and eventually he departed.

We then travelled down to Florida, hoping we could get across to Nassau in the Bahamas to catch our ship to Southampton. It was not to be as the cost was horrendous and there were problems buying a ticket 'in' but not 'out'. We already had that, of course. Fortunately our ship Himalaya was sailing into Miami, so we picked it up there.

Only the Atlantic Ocean stood between us and Mother England. Overall I had been away for about two and a half years and in the days before computers, emails and the internet, I relied on letter writing to keep in touch. Phone calls were all but kept for birthdays and Christmas, but that wasn't always totally satisfactory with a delay on the line or the volume very faint. During my travels, my mother kept every letter I wrote and later she returned them to me. They make very interesting reading and in the course of producing this book, I have been able to refer to them as something of a 'refresher', although my memories of that period remain strong.

By then, I had travelled around the world, but I had not travelled to Scotland. On arriving back in the United Kingdom, Mother and Bill took me up there for a few good days, to a lovely place called Kirkcudbright. But as usual, I came back absolutely broke and soon had to find work once again. For me, it had to be in London, but because I did not intend to stay, I moved around a bit. I rented a room in a beautiful flat in Chelsea with a friend I had previously worked with. She often held the most amazing parties, but one was particularly embarrassing for me. On this occasion I invited my cousin, Sally, to come along. At some stage during the evening my flat-friend sought me out, angrily advising that someone was in her bed with a man. She did not know the guilty woman, but it turned out that I did. It was Sally!

I then answered an advertisement for sharing another flat, this time in Kensington. Sally would come and stay and slept on the floor as nothing seemed to bother her. One day, as we were getting ready to go out, I admired her jacket, saying that I had never seen her wearing it before. Quite flippantly Sally advised that she had been through my flat-mate's wardrobe when she was out and liked the look of it. Of course it was a 'borrow' not a 'take' but it is not something I would have done.

Throughout my time overseas my brother Michael and I remained great mates. We'd keep in contact and I saw a lot of him once I arrived back home. The physical distance between us while I was travelling the world did not come between us and even though we were well and truly into adulthood by then, I felt we had remained close siblings.

I continued to correspond with Ian and it seemed he really wanted me to go back to New Zealand. Sheila was also eager to return, so we both saved for the fare and were off again. This time I could not face the long sea voyage, but Sheila seemed happy to do it, so took most of my luggage with her. I flew via Denmark, Singapore and Thailand, a short seven-night trip in comparison. I moved in with Ian. Sheila arrived a few weeks later and I remember we went down to meet the Shota Rustavelli, which had carried her safely from Southampton to Auckland. This cruise ship appeared, to us at least, to be listing heavily. Ian was very quick to suggest that must be due to my luggage being on that side.

Ian and I settled into Auckland life as a couple while Sheila stayed with Mike, who had been introduced to us by Leah. I found work with a firm of solicitors and very much enjoyed it there until the lawyer I worked for went out on his own as a barrister and Queen's Counsel. I was honoured to be asked to go with him, but I found it a bit lonely without the camaraderie of my colleagues as there was only he and I in his office. However, the work turned out to be interesting, and I met clients like Phil Warren, a promoter who brought many variety acts to New Zealand. I benefited from this as Phil gave me tickets to some of the shows.

Ian and I then rented a flat in Mount Eden. It was a small place but was most convenient, being close to the central city where we worked. One day we came home from work to find my cousin Sally on our doorstep. I had known she had set off on her big 'OE' and would arrive in Auckland at some stage, but her timing was a complete surprise. Sally introduced herself to Ian, who remembers her words to this day. 'Hello, I am Sally, Adrienne's cousin and I've come to stay'. And stay she did! I loved Sally. She was my best mate but I was under no illusion as to her character. She stayed for sure and stayed, then stayed some more. We'd take her out to bars and she would chat to us, but her eyes would be forever wandering over our shoulders towards any good looking man who walked through the door.

Our flat only had one bedroom and Sally slept on the floor so we would never know who we were going to step over in the morning. Finally we had to say it was time to get her own place, and she did - just across the road. Sally never seemed to have any money but I knew what that was like so I didn't get upset at the frequent request for loans.

One of Aunty Ruth's best friends – a bridesmaid in earlier times - was Patsy. She had come out to New Zealand with her husband and Sally and I went to look them up. Patsy became a good friend and is one to this day. She had one daughter, who lived in England, and three sons. They were a good Christian family and took us into their hearts.

By then I was well settled with Ian but they were simply brilliant with Sally. She eventually went to live with them, but Patsy had to give her a talking to as she clearly didn't give up old habits easily. Having strange men in her bed didn't impress Patsy.

Sally liked New Zealand and wanted to stay but there were problems with work permits, which had limitations on them. Every now and then she had to leave the country for a while, before returning. She was not actually entitled to work, but she often did so under an assumed name. I don't know how she got away with that but she did. Once I married Ian there was no such problem for me. I was quite disappointed with Sally when Ian and I got married because she decided she needed a stint out of New Zealand and disappeared to Australia. I would have really liked her support.

One member of the family who almost came to our wedding was Aunty Marjorie. She had visited New Zealand before to visit her cousins, Shirley and Valerie, whom I had met previously and she was planning to come out for a second visit. The dates didn't coincide but she did come to Auckland for three nights to see us and to be another member of the family to meet Ian, along with Sally, of course.

Aunt Marjorie has been a very special person in my life and we have stayed with her and vice versa. She always kept in touch by writing beautiful letters. I'll never forget some of the meals Aunt Marjorie made for us - she was the only one who could replicate the childhood memories of meals made by my Granny Lobb. Her kindness and attention were so very different from my Aunty Ruth who, I feel strongly, could have made more of an effort to stay in touch.

~ *Eight* ~

Ian and I got married on 15th November 1973 in a register office ceremony. I knew my father would not be able to come. He had met Eileen while she was married to Leslie and he got on very well with both of them. But Leslie died suddenly and Dad was there a lot to add support for Eileen. The romance blossomed, and they got married the same year as we did.

At the time of my wedding, my father was going through financial problems with the business. An employee had been stealing from him and some of his clients were letting him down quite badly regarding payments as well. It was all serious enough that he was almost broke when he married Eileen, but he was never made bankrupt. Effectively it was what they refer to as a cashflow problem, caused by what's said to be white collar pilfering, along with outright theft. But he was determined not to be pushed into bankruptcy and at least he had found happiness with Eileen after two disastrous previous marriages.

Mother and Bill declined to come to my wedding, merely sending a bunch of flowers and a set of lingerie, from where else? Yes, the lingerie came from Allens! I don't know why they didn't come and I was terribly disappointed.

My brother, as usual, was doing his own thing, as far as a military life allows. He had volunteered to join the regular Army in the Junior Leaders Regiment at the ripe old age of fifteen. Had he not done so, he would have ended up in borstal, as Dad put it.

Michael moved on to the Royal Artillery and was stationed in Germany before being selected for the 22nd Special Air Services Regiment of the British Army, the elite of the armed forces. I remember our father was terribly proud of him at the time. In those days the SAS was not so well known by the public, however now their rigorous training schedule can be found on websites. Endurance training is usually carried out in the Brecon Beacons in Wales, and I do remember my brother training there and in the jungles of Belize. In the jungle they had to learn survival in the harshest of conditions, living on minimal rations. Only a small number make it through such training and into the SAS.

I also remember hearing of the 'interrogations' my brother had to endure, specifically being dangled by the feet over a barrel of water and being dunked every so often. The mental stamina, as well as the fitness of these men was tested to the core. This training also included escape, evasion and tactical questioning.

Overall this training was to leave Michael in good stead for his future personal war – against me – as he became an expert in resisting interrogation and enduring stress.

So none of my family was at my wedding and from that perspective it wasn't what most brides dream of. Just a few friends came around for drinks and nibbles at the house Sheila and Mike shared. My friend Jenny made the beautiful wedding cake.

Ian's father and his partner were there too, as were Patsy and John. As usual we were virtually broke, and I said I would rather spend money on a honeymoon than the wedding. So after going out to dinner with a couple of friends, we set off to Fiji for our honeymoon. It sounds good, but Fiji consists of several Pacific islands and is not the idyllic paradise people in Europe would probably envisage. But we drove around the main island and thoroughly enjoyed ourselves, with a welcome break from work.

Shortly afterwards Sheila married Mike and their daughter Elizabeth duly arrived on the scene. I was delighted to be asked to be godmother. I was also keen to start a family and have a house of our own. The flat in Mount Eden was very small with a minute balcony and I missed a garden, or just somewhere to sit outside in the summer.

Although we were offered a very good deal to manage the ten apartments in our block in exchange for rent-free accommodation, we turned it down and took over Jenny's unit in Northcote. That was better; but I still deeply believed in owning one's own property. The reality for us though is that we simply could not afford to buy at that time. We just did not have enough for a deposit and didn't qualify for a State mortgage, so we decided to give it a go back in England.

Ian had never done much travelling, only to the Pacific islands and Australia and by then I was pregnant, so it was a case of now or never. We arrived in the United Kingdom in March 1975, four months before the daughter we were to name Rachel made her arrival in the world. We went to Bridlington with me wearing a mini-skirt and it was snowing. Mini-skirts were long out of fashion in Britain by then, but were all the rage in New Zealand. My mother was horrified by how I was dressed. As a permanent residence, I knew Ian would never be happy in Yorkshire as it was far too cold, but my father offered us the flat over his business premises in Dorking. Another alternative was Michael's terraced house in Durrington, near Salisbury in Wiltshire, and that was the option we settled on, mainly because of the garden.

On Boxing Day 1974 Michael had been wounded during an SAS encounter in Oman and almost lost his life. He was airlifted back to the United Kingdom to recuperate. One of his best mates, Johnny, was fatally wounded in the same attack. Michael didn't speak very much about his confrontations with the enemy but I did ask him once how he felt when he first killed someone in action. 'Nothing,' he said, shrugging his shoulders flippantly. 'It's nothing.'

Michael once gave me a special Christmas present related to his SAS encounters. It was a silver Maria Theresa dollar which the Omanis used as currency. He had it mounted and put on a chain. He said he took it from the body of a rebel he had killed. His training with the SAS stood him in good stead and he told me how he could kill with a single strike of a hand in the right place across someone's neck. I concluded then that I would not wish to be that person.

So Ian and I started our life in the United Kingdom in Michael's Durrington property. My brother had recovered from his injuries and returned to Oman so we rented the house and when he came home on leave he would come to stay with us. It worked out well in the short term, but I could not see it being so as a long-term arrangement. Michael's house had been done up very nicely and was two rooms up and three down. The kitchen was at the back, with a dining room and sitting room in the front. It also had a small garden.

Ian got a job almost immediately in Salisbury which he enjoyed although it was a very different way of working to what he was used to.

Rachel Elizabeth Nairn was born on 16th July 1975. There was no reason why we picked the name Rachel other than that we liked it, but Elizabeth, on the other hand, maintained a family tradition. I was Elizabeth, so was my mother and I think she may have acquired that name from Aunt Lily.

My father and Eileen were the first people to visit Rachel and I in the maternity hospital. Eileen may only have been a step-grandmother to Rachel, but she turned out to be a wonderful granny. Rachel called her Gran, just as she called my mother's husband, Bill, Grandpa. She had two wonderful sets of grandparents in England.

Jane and her new boyfriend Mike were our second visitors. They eventually married and had two children, Simon and Debbie. I was delighted to be asked to Debbie's godmother, but tragically Jane was to die from pancreatic cancer when her daughter was just 14 years old, but Mike was to remain a good friend and feature strongly in our lives.

Mother and Bill left it for a couple of weeks before visiting and in September we took Rachel to Bridlington to be christened. We had serious thoughts about her godparents as I had been disappointed with mine, only really knowing my Aunty Judy.

My mother had always told me to have relations. 'They will always be there for you,' she said. Actually I did want my cousin Sally to fill one role as godmother to Rachel. The best laid plans of mice and men! Sally's sister, Madeleine however pressed me, almost begging me to name her. She was so keen and at that time Sally was settled in New Zealand, having married John. It seemed sensible to have one godmother in England, as the other was always going to be my old friend Sheila. I truly thought Madeleine would be a good godmother. We opted to make my brother her godfather, with Bill standing in at the christening as Michael was abroad as usual. Mother put on a lovely spread for us all and it was a beautiful family gathering.

We were back in Bridlington for Christmas that year and during lunch at Aunty Ruth's my grandmother made rather a nasty comment. I was finding it difficult eating lunch and holding Rachel at the same time when Grandmother snapped 'It's no good looking disgruntled Adrienne, we've all had to bounce babies on our knees.' Still the one to keep my mouth shut, I refrained from telling her she was wrong, she had never bounced a baby on her knee while eating lunch – she always had nannies! Even when Michael was born, my mother had the services of a nanny, the old family servant who helped her out.

But again we were struggling financially and I was missing my salary. We couldn't even afford a decent pram – Allens didn't sell such things - so there was nothing left to do but go back to work, which I did when Rachel was five months old. I obtained a position with a firm of solicitors in Salisbury and got a good baby minder in Durrington to look after her. Anne absolutely adored Rachel, as did her two girls, and she was well looked after. But it was hard work and long days

Those solicitors in Salisbury did me a great disservice, one that was to have far-reaching effects many years later. At that time married women could opt to pay a reduced National Insurance contribution, and all the pros and cons were supposed to be explained to us. I remember distinctly being told by these solicitors that it was most advantageous for all married women to pay the reduced contributions as any future benefits could be claimed through our husbands' contributions except unemployment benefit. As I had never had any trouble getting a job, I felt this was a minor consideration.

However, in my particular case there was a double-edged blow. Because my husband didn't work his full employable age in the United Kingdom, he would only be entitled to sixty per cent of the pension to be paid out by that country on retirement.

In essence this meant that I would only ever be entitled to sixty per cent of my husband's sixty per cent. On the basis of bad information, and in my case, inadequate information, provided by my employer I made a very bad choice and it proved to be far from advantageous. The pros and cons had in fact been set out clearly in a leaflet, but I was never given that document by my employers, who were, after all solicitors!

All this dawned on me in later years and, as I thought many married women would be in the same position, I wrote many letters to many different departments, as well as our local Member of Parliament. It was, of course, to no avail. I was categorically told I would have signed a form at the time, which I did, and I would have been handed a leaflet by my employers explaining all of the implications. I most certainly was not handed that leaflet and I question how anyone could insist every employer throughout the United Kingdom fulfilled this requirement. But there was to be no compromise and I am now suffering the consequences.

We always knew we would not be able to stay indefinitely in my brother's house. When he came home on leave he always wanted to check that the house was in a spotless condition, literally. He would run his fingers along the tops of doors to check for dirt or dust – it was a standing joke at that time. So we knew we would have to be out of the house by the time Rachel began drawing on walls!

One day we took a drive to Warminster, about 20 miles away, and by chance happened to see some show homes on a new housing estate. We walked into one of the houses and came out having bought it. It cost us £10,000 and we were just amazed we could afford it. I had always had a small account with the Halifax Building Society and went to them for a mortgage, but we were refused. However Leeds Permanent came up trumps although we had never had any dealings with that business. There was a special deal where the builders covered the solicitor's costs, which was about £200. I did not have a solicitor so I phoned my Aunty Ruth and she said she was sure Uncle Trevor's firm would act for us. Thankfully I did not get a bill as he got the £200 from the builders.

We moved in during May 1976, one of the hottest summers on record at the time. The previous summer had also been very hot – I certainly knew all about it, having spent most of it being pregnant. Ian was beginning to wonder what all the fuss was about in relation to England's 'bad' weather. Our new house was a four up and two down affair, with the kitchen and sitting room downstairs and three bedrooms and a bathroom upstairs. In subsequent years we added on a garage, a separate dining room, a sun room and later, a rumpus room for Rachel above the garage.

As we were both working in Salisbury at that time, we made the drive to Durrington every day to leave Rachel, went on to work and then back home via Durrington again. It was a tiring journey and made for a long day so I searched for a job in Warminster and came up with something at a plastic bag factory. It was not going to the most exciting of jobs and I thought the salary was terrible, so I initially turned it down. But there was nothing else and the job centre advised me this was a good salary for Warminster. So I went back to see the employer – with my tail between my legs and with baby Rachel on my shoulder. Just before my appointment, Rachel threw up on me, but my potential boss was sympathetic and fortunately the job was still available. I accepted the position.

Ian got a job with West Wilt District Council, travelling to Melksham every day and after a few false starts we got a good minder for Rachel.

By then things were beginning to work out for us, although Mother knew we were usually short of money. Bill still worked for the Midland Bank, where we had an account, and knew our circumstances. At one stage the manager mentioned to him that maybe it would be best if we moved our account as we were always overdrawn and Mother passed this message on to us. Of course Bill should never have told her as banking matters were always considered to be strictly confidential.

At the plastic bag factory one of the men was aware that I did not find the work interesting, so he told me his wife worked for NatWest and her manager needed a new secretary. She arranged an appointment, I got the job and off I went to work for NatWest. I stayed there for 22 years. My boss was an old-style bank manager, a relic of times long gone and a real gentleman. It was a requirement that all staff bank with NatWest, so the Midland manager got his wish, being happy, I am sure, when we moved our account.

But tragedy was to strike us as a family. Sally came to visit with her husband, but on arrival in the United Kingdom she told John she did not want to be with him any longer and she left him to his own devices. We saw her and she loved Rachel to bits, but she returned to New Zealand to continue her job with Air New Zealand.

She had only been back there for two weeks when she had a car accident driving home from an early morning flight and was killed instantly. Although separated, John brought her ashes back to England and we went up to Bridlington for the funeral. It was a family-only affair and I was so sad, having been through a lot with my cousin over the course of our lives. Aunty Ruth was devastated as one would expect. I suspected she was hoping Sally and John would get back together to give her grandchildren.

I had known Sally had had a couple of terminated pregnancies before she married and on one occasion my mother and Bill drove her back from London to Bridlington after such a procedure, but I don't think they ever divulged this to Aunty Ruth. Secrets have been kept in our family, as they are in most families. A person keeps secrets for a reason and usually that's because to divulge the truth would be very hurtful and I am sure this was the case with Mother and Bill in relation to Sally.

~ *Nine* ~

Another big thing happened to our family in 1977, with the doors being closed for the last time at Allens. My mother had been running the business since my grandfather died and Uncle Trevor insisted that her husband, Bill would 'go into Allens over my dead body.' That didn't concern Bill as he didn't want to have anything to do with Allens anyway. Aunty Ruth only lasted about a week working there, so there was no-one left in the family to take over. The times were well on the way to changing, with that type of shop being seen as too old fashioned.

The other big store which competed directly with Allens in Bridlington was Carltons. In my family's eyes at least Carltons was very much the underdog, being down-market and in the wrong part of town. But the family which owned Carltons did very well for itself, selling out to Binns, the big department store operator from Hull. Carltons may have disappeared as a family-run business, but its location in Chapel Street soon became more central to Bridlington than the Promenade where Allens was situated. As a result, Allens was sold off at a rock-bottom price to Underwoods, a down-market store.

The former Allens building was then subjected to a major change. All the fixtures and fittings went to auction, with all Grandfather's beautiful big clocks going under the hammer. He had loved clocks and his favourites were the big grandfather pieces. While he was alive he would do the rounds at Allens every morning winding them up and checking the time against his pocket watch. My cousin Nic requested one of these clocks, but he had to go to the auction and bid for it. It was a sad year 1977 – truly the end of the Allens era.

As previously noted, my brother and I had always had an excellent relationship. Perhaps the trauma of our parents' divorce when we were young brought us closer together, or maybe it was just that Michael thought he ought to be protective of his only sister, at least where others were involved. But I know at that time, we were good friends, not just siblings.

After the SAS and a stint in Angola in the diamond mines on the security side of things, Michael had joined the Sultan of Oman's Forces as a mercenary. He knew a career in that part of the world would be hugely lucrative, having served there previously in the SAS. For him, money was the greatest draw card.

When Ian, Rachel and I moved to Warminster, Michael decided it was time for him to move and he bought a house in our little town too. This turned out to be convenient as we were able to look out for him, to check his mail if he was away and to make sure his bills were paid on time.

To keep the communications going, we began to make audio tapes, which we would send to each other. Our father made some too, sending them to my brother also, and vice versa. They were great tapes, chit chatty in discussing almost everything we did. I have a number of them to this day.

Ian and I got on extremely well with Dad and his wife Eileen and saw a lot of them. But Michael didn't like Eileen at all. He made the pretence of getting on with her, but Dad knew what he really felt.

Eileen was forever matchmaking in a bid to set my brother Michael up with her younger relations, a second cousin in particular. Michael didn't actually need any help, as he managed quite well in finding girlfriends under his own steam. He had many and we met a lot of them. Sarah was one, a lovely person, and they went out for quite a while. But she broke it off suddenly, much to our surprise. The account came back to us, through Nic's wife Jenny, that Sarah was scared of him, for whatever reason.

Lyn seemed quite serious too. She was a chiropodist and a friend of Jenny's also. We really thought something would come of it as Michael and Lyn chose a house in Rockbourne, in the New Forest, to renovate. Michael was really tempted to take on the housing development market, because Nic and Jenny were having success doing just that. So he bought the Rockbourne house. He never lived in it however and I don't think any work was ever carried out on that house because the relationship with Lyn came to an abrupt end when Penny arrived on the scene.

Michael met Penny in Oman where she was also working. Understandably she was not interested in a house Michael had chosen with someone else, although it was only ever in his name. Before long it was sold.

Penny endeared herself to all the members of our family and it was obvious she wanted to marry Michael. Not only was it obvious, but she told us all - my cousins, Madeleine, Nic, Jenny, myself. She tried to get us to convince Michael it was time to settle down. By this time he was in his late thirties and Penny a year older and we thought if they wanted to have children, they would have to get a move on. Penny's plan worked a treat, and they were married in Oman in 1983.

But if we thought there would be wedding invitations all round, we were to be disappointed. Dad was hugely excited with anticipation of being invited and was so disappointed not to be. Michael's reason for not inviting his father was that he didn't want to be embarrassed by Eileen. His comments were even more hurtful, saying 'everyone knows she is stupid so why does she have to open her mouth to prove it.'

I expected Rachel at least to be asked to be a bridesmaid, but to be fair, like our wedding, that was not the style. Once again it was a register office wedding and while I believe Penny's mother attended, I am not sure of that. Michael and Penny kept pretty quiet about it and it was never mentioned.

While they were away in Oman, we continued to look after Michael's house in Warminster. We also did anything else he asked. One humorous incident occurred at that time. On this occasion Michael sent an audio tape to me and enclosed a cheque for £10. Penny was on holiday at home in England without him at the time and I just mentioned to her on the phone that I had received a tape. But I hadn't had time to listen to the tape before telling her there was a cheque for £10 enclosed. Immediately Penny said that the cheque would be for flowers for her. So there it was – she was right – me and my big mouth. I had to order flowers for Penny. In the tape, Michael described the purpose.

I am enclosing a £10 cheque. I wonder if you could please order from Interflora the summer special I have seen advertised in the Punch magazine. The summer special is a bouquet of pink carnations and pink roses, I believe. They cost £9.99, if you can manage that super. If you can't manage that Adrienne, you know, just flowers of your choice, whatever one can get for £10. I don't know but if you could get them delivered to my wife with suitable greetings of 'Miss you Sweetheart my ever-loving wife.' No, I think 'miss you sweetheart' would be better. I haven't done anything wrong, there's no apology to go with it, so just 'miss you sweetheart.' If you could do that I would be very grateful.

Later, I replied, in a subsequent tape, saying:-

You've heard about my blunder. I'm ever so sorry. I really am. That's the trouble with me Michael I'm so open. I just tell everyone everything without realising.

Michael's response was:-

Well my little sister, your blunder, enough said. It's a pity, I would have liked to have given her a surprise but I'll do it some other time. No problem at all. Thanks for putting the money in the bank. Splendid. To answer your question as to why you are not told everything... enough said on that subject I think...

But everything was not always so lovely-dovey in the Michael and Penny Lobb household. They were both home on leave when I got a telephone call one evening from a very hysterical and obviously deeply distressed Penny. She was screaming down the phone alleging that Michael was trying to kill her. I was horrified and immediately informed Ian, saying that we had better go over their right away.

Ian didn't move, simply advising that we should 'let Michael get on it.' My husband has a great perception of people and I know he didn't like Penny's motives a lot of the time. But deep down, he didn't really believe Michael would kill her. There was not a lot I could do on my own, but I did phone later to see if all was okay. Things had obviously settled and their marital problem, whatever it was, had been diffused. We didn't mention it again.

~ *Ten* ~

At some stage Bill had a spot of bother as my mother called it. It was Bill's practice to walk to the bank every morning by same route, at the same time. He always strolled along with a walking stick, smoking his pipe, and wearing a long raincoat and hat. He cut an old fashioned figure.

However friends of the family accused Bill of following their young daughter. She was frightened of him and I believe the Police were called but there was no evidence or anything that amounted to proof. Uncle Trevor, a solicitor, wrote a letter to that family, telling them to stop making false accusations. Nothing more was ever heard of the matter but Bill certainly had the unpleasant experience of being accused of something he did not do, something I was to encounter later in my life.

Granny Allen died in 1986, the last of my grandparents. We always expected to be around when our grandparents died and it was taken in our stride, although I was very upset about all of their deaths when they happened.

When Granny Lobb died she left the sum of £100 to each of her three grandchildren. That was a great amount of money in those days and was totally unexpected as far as I was concerned.

Granny and Grandpa Allen had moved from their large house at 86 Cardigan Road in Bridlington to a flat attached to the Expanse Hotel. It was very nice and had a lovely view of the beach and the Esplanade. Grandmother had beautiful furniture, including several grandfather clocks tucked well and truly away from the clutches of the Allens store auctioneers as they were privately owned.

Mother and Aunty Ruth were the beneficiaries of the estate. None of my three cousins - Richard's children - nor Aunty Judy got any mention in Granny Allen's will. I thought this was unfair as surely her deceased son's children should also have a share. But Uncle Trevor, the solicitor, had drawn up the will and that stipulated everything was to go my mother and Ruth. Michael was later to relate that he felt Uncle Trevor had made sure he got the lion's share.

I remember going up to Bridlington for the funeral, as did all the grandchildren. Michael and Penny were home on leave and were looking to move back to the United Kingdom permanently. They were at that time looking at Napton Windmill, a property as grand as it sounded, with a swimming pool on the ground floor of the windmill area. However Michael did not seem keen. He always weighed up the pros and cons and would not commit. So when we were all in Bridlington for Granny Allen's funeral, Penny used the opportunity to get the family onside again in a bid to persuade him the windmill property was a good buy. Jenny in particular, with expertise in property, was roped in and, once again, Penny was successful.

My father was not so keen on the idea and tried to point out the heavy workload which would be involved with such a property. But expressing those concerns probably swayed stubborn Michael to buy.

Michael later described that time to me in one of his audio tapes.

I mentioned we were looking for a house other than Warminster to Dad, and he said he still had the plans of Ashbury, the bungalow at Ifield. I mean Adrienne, it really was very small – only two bedrooms and I did say, not exactly short, but probably shorter than I could have been or should have been, I said I wasn't really looking for a bungalow which I wasn't. I said I had sold Rockbourne at a profit but not quite as much of a profit as if I had put the money in stocks and shares.

Michael had told me Dad had responded by saying:-

You should have bought a plot and I offered you the plans of Ashbury, but you pooh -poohed them.

Michael went on to say to me:-

I mean you can't really compare Rockbourne with Ashbury and unfortunately I think I have found whatever conversation one has with Dad, he always reverts to what he had got in mind to tell you anyway. So you can talk about roses or whatever and if he has pre-planned in his mind that he is going to tell you about the bungalow, he would say 'those roses there are lovely. They would look nice in front of a bungalow wouldn't they?' And get back on the subject again. The Mill, yes I am aware of what is involved and I shall ha·

to see how it goes, but I am in full possession of the facts. Wrong. I think I am in full possession of the facts, but Dad is nowhere near in full possession of the facts. I know how much money I've got, how much money we've got and I know the state of our finances and I won't say I think we can afford it but we are going to have a go at it. What I do find mildly irritating is the fact that Dad, who hasn't seen the Windmill and who hasn't even looked at the details or weighed it up – this factor of money has come into his mind which, I accept is very important, but he focuses on one thing without looking at the other points as mitigating circumstances. But the point that irritated me particularly was he said 'the maintenance - you will be forever working on it, painting this and doing that and so on and so forth. You'll get fed up with it.' No he didn't say I would get fed up with it.

Michael suddenly checked himself in realisation.

He said 'I wonder if you have considered the maintenance for a property such as you have described. I think it will be considerable and you will have to spend an awful long time in your routine just maintaining it.' And then in the very next sentence he says 'I find the garden almost more than I can cope with now. People have urged us to move into a flat or something but I won't do it. I like the garden we like the views and I am prepared to put up with it.' You know, he answered my question. Well not my question I mean he has answered my problem. You weigh up the pros and cons and you decide whether you are prepared to accept them. He is prepared to accept the garden, which I think is foolishness.

He then added:-

And I would further argue the case that he is mucking around with his health while we are only mucking around with money. Not quite a very good analogy, but I would be far happier to see Dad in a flat. I think it would be better off for both of them. I really do. The bungalow I can remember Dad telling me some time ago several years ago, that it was worth £50,000 I think. I would have thought in the Worthing area now, after the rises this year, it would be worth £70/75,000. I would have thought that would be minimal. I would rather say £80,000 give or take £10,000 either way. I mean if you are talking about money why doesn't he move to a flat, a cheaper property and have a greater income coming in?

My brother did show concerns for my father's health, and his own.

I am concerned about Dad. He is getting old now, and whereas Eileen is the younger of the two, I really don't think she is going to be an awful lot of good assisting looking after Dad. I think he spends more of his time looking after her with her toes or whatever it is she's got. I don't know. I am extremely irritated with Eileen. I am quite annoyed. When I phoned from the airport as I always phone from the airport, to be leaving the country to be told by Eileen that she thinks Dad needs a by-pass operation, I didn't, in all honesty, worry all the way back on the aircraft, because there was absolutely nothing I could have done about it but I sat on the aircraft and I thought 'what am I going to do?' I mean I phoned Penny immediately afterwards and tipped her off. But I sat on the aircraft and thought what can I do? And I thought I can do nothing. There is nothing I can do. In that case leave it. Don't worry about it, and I haven't worried about it. I have been concerned about it. You appreciate the difference.

He goes on to add:-

I think it was an extremely irresponsible phone call. I really do. To wait for me to call, and then hit me with that at the airport as I fly out. If the thing had been of that great concern, why hadn't they phoned me at home anyway. Why didn't they say 'we know you're not coming round, but there are a couple of things I think we need to talk about'. Dad's future does concern me.

While Granny Allen's financial assets were split between my mother and Aunty Ruth, there was a lot of furniture to be dealt with and after my mother and aunty had made their choice as to what they wanted, I was offered some items. I did feel really bad about being given first pickings, knowing that Michael and Penny were away.

Michael told me:-

Adrienne, please don't worry about Granny's things and you getting in first and Penny not going or what have you. It really is no problem at all.

He then went on to explain:-

Having said that, you then describe the paintings and funnily enough I quite like the painting, the Woodland Grove. I have sat and looked at that for hours but if Penny doesn't like it or any of the paintings, then I don't suppose there is a lot of point. Although I don't think it's so much whether you like the painting itself, it's the memories if evokes for you. I quite liked it. The tapestry, super, the larger one, whatever, that's fine. Back to the paintings again, we have got so many pictures and picture frames, we have got hundreds and hundreds and hundreds – we've got stacks of them. Funnily enough the windmill isn't particularly suited to pictures. Very difficult to hang pictures in a windmill. Even on the straight walls in fact – there are lots of windows and things and there isn't a great wall expanse.

The Woodland Grove picture, I don't think Penny likes it. We really need to get things we both like. I only like it for association of ideas – my association of memories. I remembered it for years and years and years sitting above the chimney piece at Belvedere Road and I can remember getting into the picture, so to speak. I quite like it, but anyway, we shall have to see.

Rocking chairs. A rocking chair is one thing. A collection of rocking chairs is something entirely different. Yes, I would quite like a rocking chair; but Adrienne, we will sort this out when I get home. I really have no hard and fast rules, whatsoever, on any of this. Mother kept Granny's good stuff, well good for her. The fighting cocks. Yes, I have already got fighting cocks. I wish I had known as they are better than mine. I'm not all that keen on them now. I have gone off them; but never mind, that's the way it goes.

The bed, yes, we are interested in the king size bed. You said the three piece suite, was Granny Woodmansey's. I thought it was the three piece suite, Mother's three piece suite, the one in the sitting room by the television. I'm sure that wasn't Granny Woodmansey's. I may have got it wrong, whatever. Yes, furnishing for the windmill, it might be handy to have something until we can get or afford furniture we really want. I find it very difficult while I am in Oman to project my thoughts back to Europe and to envisage things and see things. It really does encourage one to become a schizophrenic. Life here and life back there and ne'er the twain shall meet. The furniture, quite honestly Adrienne, it would be nice to have something to remind me of Granny, it might be convenient to have some furniture as a make do until we can get the furniture of our choice. How much did you pay Mother for them? Was it an agreeable rate or whatever?

My brother liked to put a price on everything. In fact this time, my mother was actually giving the things away. After all, she had been given them by Granny. Michael accused our father of being money conscious, but he had his own ideas:-

Your new car. Yes I know what you mean. I think the XR2 is a very sensible choice. I know what Ian means about having just that little bit more power. I fully agree and with regard to the garage, a smaller car makes a lot of sense. Is it narrow? I thought the problem with the garage was the width. It certainly is shorter. I would be interested to know just how much room there is, but I suppose when you are short of room every inch and a half or whatever it is counts. Yes, sounds a good choice. It sounds a good buy and I am very pleased. I think it is very good. I didn't quite get the full details of the price, you said a basic XR2 was £6750 and one with all the extras on it was £7100 and you were getting one with all the extras for £6,000 was it? I didn't quite get the bit what you got back for your car, was it £3450 in the end. Not sure what I would get for the MG. It is a pity, but funnily enough, I think the problem with the MG has been Dutton Forshaws. I don't know what you know about them as a garage but basically the MG has got a first-class engine.
It is a superb engine and it will last for years and years and years, although in fact I have got through three exhausts in six years because it is laid up for so long.

He then corrects himself:-

Wrong. I have got through two exhausts. It's on the third exhaust now. But the MG should last for years and years, but because I got it new I wanted an electronic ignition on it and I wanted the electric windows and sun roof and the other things put in and the problem

- two problems I have had with the MG – one was it kept stopping and that was traced to the electronic ignition which Dutton Forshaw put in and then, as you know, as Penny will never forget, we nearly had a fire driving down from Bridlington and that was caused by the wire in the electric windows through the heater controls again put in by Dutton Forshaw.

I've got absolutely no claim on the garage, but everything else has stemmed from that. I gather that you probably now know the window wipers packed up on Penny but that is an electrical fault which was subsequent to the complete electrical burn-out plus the fact that John Green didn't really finish off the rewiring job because I wanted to bring it back with me before I left the country. Anyway, so I think the car itself is an extremely good car but I appreciate Penny's feelings. But I really don't think there is any point in persevering with it if Penny doesn't like it. So we may well be changing it. It's a pity because I have now had it six years and the depreciation on it now is so low that I won't actually be making money on it if you know what I mean. But the depreciation on it now makes it a cost per year so every year I can keep it now, the running costs would be proportionately cheaper in spite of the money I have spent on repairs; but I certainly accept that it is not a practical car. Anyway, we are looking for something but I am not quite sure what. I'll take that decision when I come back on leave.

And more on the subject of money from my brother's perspective:-

I certainly make a distinction between losing £350 and failing to make £350. I think there is a difference there. I don't think I am justifying my own position. As far as Rockbourne is concerned, I made money but if I had done something else with my money, I would have made more, so I failed to make more money. I didn't actually lose money on it. I think there is a difference.

I wasn't to realise until much later how important such a distinction was coming from my brother. But I did realise then how calculating he was, certainly where money – particularly obtaining money - was concerned.

~ *Eleven* ~

My father and Eileen bought a flat in Spain. The idea at one time was perhaps to go and live there for my father's health, but Eileen didn't want to on a permanent basis. They did go out for long periods in the English winter and loved it all the same. We had use of the flat for one holiday, taking Rachel, and we thoroughly enjoyed it.

When they decided to sell the flat eventually it became very difficult as there were no buyers, but a deal was struck with a former British footballer. He didn't have all the money, but he was able to pay a deposit and then the balance by instalments.

I remember it was difficult to transfer money out of Spain at that time, so my father was paid in cash. He put it in a hold-all bag and then together with Eileen and another couple caught a bus to Gibraltar. The hold-all – and its valuable contents – was put on the floor of the bus and when the Customs officials came on board to check, it was pushed under the seat between the couples. It was obviously a risky tactic, but they made it through and the cash was then lodged in a bank in Gibraltar.

But while getting the cash for the deposit out of Spain had been a breeze, getting the rest of the money from the footballer was an entirely different story. Some instalments were made, but often they had to chase him up at times for more. I know my father never did recover the whole amount, which made him angry as he loathed all debts, particularly unpaid ones.

Eileen had an aunt by marriage who lived with her sister, Doris. Dad and Eileen did a lot for these two sisters and when the aunt died they helped with clearing the house and looking after the estate, going so far as to move Doris into a bungalow just down the road from them in Findon. They continued to do everything for Doris but it proved to be too much as this very wealthy lady began to take advantage of their goodwill.

It came to a head when Doris phoned Eileen to ask her to arrange a hair appointment for her. That was the last straw as far as my father was concerned and Eileen told Doris she should be doing that sort of thing herself. It proved to be the end of their relationship!

I suppose with hindsight small things can really make or break relationships. One such incident occurred in 1986, when I had a major argument with my mother. By then Ian and I had got ourselves on our feet financially, but one day I had a major cash flow crisis. I had forgotten about quite a large direct debit, about £4000, but the bank paid it, causing our account to become overdrawn. In those days staff accounts were not allowed be overdrawn, so I was in a spot of bother. I had the money in the form of investments to cover the bill, but needed to sell some shares in order to extinguish the overdraft. But that was going to take time, and time is something I did not have.

As one would, I asked Mother if she could lend us the money, knowing she had just come into about £35,000 by way of her inheritance from my Granny Allen. Mother had always had huge financial support from her parents, but to my utter shock and surprise, she rejected my request, speaking more than a little sharply in doing so. That was it - no negotiation. I expressed my feelings about that in the heat of the moment with words that could not be taken back.

Luckily, Michael came to our aid. I had told him it would be for about a month until our money came and I remember clearly even before the deadline, he was asking for the return of the money he had loaned us.

The good relationship which had always existed between Mother and I broke down simply because I asked her to help out in the very short-term. She was really quite brutal in how she responded to what would, in the circumstances, have been a usual request within such a close family circle.

For five years neither of us phoned each other. We were both to blame really, but what surprised me was how little my brother did to rectify the situation. He didn't try to broker a form of reconciliation and indeed never mentioned the impasse as far as I can recall.

Rachel had developed serious health problems in the form of psoriasis at that time and Ian and I saw this problem as taking precedence over all else, from our perspective. However, my cousin Nic did step in and try to smooth things over between mother and myself. He and Jenny were wonderful friends. Nic however did like a drink and sometimes he would imbibe late into the night, which would get him thinking about things. About two in the morning Nic phoned me to advise, sternly, that the dissent between my mother and I had gone on long enough. He had phoned her too, delivering a similar message.

It was me however – Adrienne the peacemaker - who phoned my

mother and made up. After that phone call everything was put behind us. It really had gone on too long.

Our relationship with my father and Eileen was always strong. He was always willing to help in any way he could and he did so when Ian and I got into an argument with a travel company over a bad holiday we'd had.

My father had been in Court on a number of occasions, fighting battles with companies and individuals regarding bad debts and he usually acted for himself. He was one to always stand up for himself and his rights, so he encouraged me to take the travel company to Court. He came along to support me, but the company didn't even bother to send a representative so I won the case.

I remember my brother saying he would never end up like our father, fighting battles in Court. Michael prefers to fight for his rights out of Court. It's macho and brave to be the Provocateur!

Rachel's health problem had begun with chickenpox. But the spots did not go away and when I took her to the doctor he diagnosed psoriasis. I had never heard of it; but we soon found out a lot. Basically it is incurable, but not contagious. She had it badly, her torso was covered, with patches on her arms and legs, and her scalp was covered with a thick crust – so thick in fact it cracked. The most common relief was a Betnovate cream and plenty of sun. Basically it is a condition you have to learn to live with. But Rachel was only about ten or eleven at that time and it affected her deeply.

We tried everything to cure Rachel of her affliction – creams, Dead Sea salts, acupuncture, Chinese herbs. You name it, we tried it. Jen even suggested a chiropractor could help and recommended a friend of hers who practised in Brockenhurst. So we embarked on that treatment path. Three times a week after school and work, Rachel and I would take the train to Southampton, then change and take another to Brockenhurst. We would then visit the chiropractor, before making the return trip. It was exhausting. Eventually we reduced the visits to once a week, but getting assistance from the chiropractor didn't do any good. If any cure or relief for her was to be found it would have been worth everything we paid out, but eventually we deduced this was just another money-making ruse by a charlatan.

Rachel spent a month in hospital in Bath, coming home at the weekends. She was having cream and sun bed treatment and was wrapped in bandages all the time. School was a problem because she used to make excuses not to go, especially on gym days. I remember the mistress would ask her embarrassingly in front of the class 'what's your excuse not to do gym today Rachel?' She knew of course, but fortunately their house-master, who happened to be the father of a good friend of mine, stepped in. He suffered from psoriasis too and supported Rachel, saying if she had any problems she was to go directly to him. There is no known cure for psoriasis, but we were able to get it under control eventually.

In 1987 my father and Eileen bought a luxury penthouse in Milford-on-Sea, a delightful little coastal village overlooking the Isle of Wight. They registered it in Eileen's name only as my father had cancer by then and he knew his time might be short.

The relationship Dad and Eileen had with my brother and his wife was not good. This was demonstrated once when Michael and Penny invited them to see the Windmill for the first time. Dad and Eileen were staying with Eileen's cousin Ted and his wife Janet and my father decided, rightly or wrongly, to take their hosts with them.

Expecting only Dad and Eileen for coffee, Penny charged out of the Windmill, yelling aggressively, with Michael in tow as the car they were travelling in reached the gate. She had not noticed our father and Eileen in the back of the car and when Michael observed them, she declared she was not expecting 'you lot'. Dad was totally embarrassed at the hostile reception, saying later it was not a very happy experience.

My brother was by no means friendly toward Eileen. He had very high expectations of people and took to showing great exception if they didn't act in the way he expected them to.

One of his audio tapes captures this sentiment well. In it he talks of Eileen and one of his best friends, Hugh, who shared his accommodation in Oman:-

Have I seen Hugh? No I haven't seen Hugh. I don't know, you know relationships change when you get married. You keep up with some people and you don't keep up with others. Hugh let me down very badly. It is not a matter of opinion. He told me he was moving out and assured me he was moving out face-to-face and he then did exactly the opposite. And, even if he had changed his mind, he didn't come back and tell me about it and I felt particularly badly about it because Penny said 'Are you sure Hugh is moving?' I said 'Hugh has told me that he is moving and let's leave it at that'. Penny said 'Well I don't think he is.' And I said 'well he told me he is. So that's it.'

Michael went on.

Then a short time later after Hugh and I had been living together on a daily basis Penny showed me a list and said 'I told you he wasn't moving.' And there was his name on the list to stay put. Now, I accosted Hugh with it and he said 'Oh well, yes'. He talked his way around it and I said 'Hugh I'm not interested. Why didn't you tell me?' I felt such a fool having stuck up for him. Not against Penny. But taking Hugh's side and supporting Hugh and he let me down so badly. I mean there are two sides to every story but I promise you Hugh hasn't got a leg to stand on. I have seen them around and I have been polite to them, but I'm afraid I really have very little to say to Hugh which I think is unfortunate considering I was best man at their wedding. I think she is frightful. I really do. I think she [Hugh's wife] is dreadful. She reminds me of Eileen.

So it turned out Michael liked things to be black and white. That's Army training for you. He was always right no matter what. Hugh was wrong and over such a little thing, Michael ended the friendship.

Michael's opinions on life in Oman were also very interesting:-

Right on with the news, I suppose. I think most of the news is connected with the economic crisis. You know the Arab countries are going through severe economic crises at the moment. The total budget depends on oil. The budget was worked out and is connected to the oil price of $20 per barrel and oil, for the most part of this year, has been round about $12 per barrel. Things are, I'm not saying gloomy for the Arab world, but it is difficult. Okay so you have to change the budget and I'm afraid the Arabs have never ever had this type of crisis before and they are not very good at things like economy and all the other associated things. They find it very difficult to make sensible economies.

They don't understand the staffing of hospitals and the fact that there is no point in having an X-ray department if you can't afford to pay radiologists and the others. They have got to cut back on ex patriots because ex-patriots are expensive to employ, houses, cars and all the other bits and pieces because everything is provided for us. Water and electricity bills are quite horrendous out here because of air conditioning. I have got four air conditioners in this house here.

Most people have air conditioning going all the time which is another thing about economists. The Royal Oman Police decided that part of their economy would be to turn off every other air conditioner, which they have done; but did not turn down the thermostat so all the other air conditioners had to work doubly hard to maintain the temperature, which meant the maintenance on those increased. So the total saving was either nothing or in fact they probably ended up with a higher maintenance bill from the air conditioning systems. So it didn't really work at all.

Michael kept secrets too. When he was considering leaving Oman he played his cards very tight to his chest. He certainly made a point that he never did anything that was not going to be for his own good.

But Penny says not to put personal news on tape. Well that is absolutely true because you never really know where tapes end up. Please don't feel miffed that I haven't kept you fully in the picture because quite honestly the picture has been changing so rapidly that it has been difficult to decide one thing because I have found out more about something else soon afterwards which changes it. Believe you me, I thought I had it all taped and I didn't. Things really have changed. All I can say at this stage is that my personal circumstances have now changed. I'm married and I have got a broader responsibility than I had before and I am trying to get the best possible deal to fulfil those responsibilities. And it may mean, in fact it will mean, a change in the situation here. The only thing I can say is ... you know me ... but rest assured that I am not throwing everything into the wind. I am being extremely certain, very certain indeed, that if I move or change my circumstances here that I have got it all cut and dried and sewn up before I actually make the move. I really have. Beyond that, I can't really say at this stage. I will give you the full details when I come on leave, because things haven't changed yet and they are not cut and dried.

His commentary continued:-

I am playing a low profile. I am not telling Dad. And I'm not telling Mother yet until I have got everything sorted out because the fewer people who know about it the better. So I am sorry I can't really give you any more details on that on the tape. All in good time when things change I will let you know. I will let you know before everybody else. Okay. But if you can keep it low key as far as Mother and Bill and Dad and Eileen are concerned because I haven't actually done anything yet and I am negotiating for the best possible position. Certainly as things are turning out I should be considerably better off both immediately and in the future. So fingers crossed and hope for the best.

My father always suspected my brother of being a Mason when in fact he wasn't. Our step-father Bill certainly was. Dad had acquired a toasting fork from a car boot sale or somewhere and suggested Michael might like it. It had the Masonic symbol on the handle.

Michael later described the scenario:-

The toasting fork that Dad gave me. I think I've already given it to Bill. I'm sure I've already given it to Bill. I think I paid Dad for it actually. I can't remember. I'm afraid the memory of Dad automatically comes with that sort of image to mind. How much did I pay? Now that you mention it, of course he was absolutely right. I mean - to me, it was just a toasting fork, and, as you described, he had his hand over the end and he just about handed it to me with his hand on the handle and then he held it toward me and revealed the square and compass at the top. As soon as I saw that, I thought, 'what a super present for Bill' and as opposed to saying 'no', I said 'yes'; but I'm afraid Dad just drew the wrong conclusion.

I suppose really he doesn't know that Bill rips his clothes off and leaps around the living room shrieking 'Boshom, Boshom'. Actually it is rather irritating because the one thing I did want, as you well know, but I will repeat as I have started, was that chain of Grandpa Lobb's, the watch chain and charm which was the five pointed star of Grandpa Lobb's that Dad gave to me, and, because I kept it in the cabinet with all the trophies, I had the third line down in his cabinet, he then gave it to Eileen. That is the Masonic Star. Not that Grandpa Lobb was a Mason.

He then added:-

I was – what's the word – disappointed. I have just had a letter from

Mother. I think Mother told me that Ruth and Trevor had gone down to - or was it Penny who told me – they had done a mammoth trip and they had dropped some stuff of Granny's off at Nic and Jen's including Grandpa Allen's old watch. I always admired Grandpa Allen's old watch, but I fully accept that it should go to Nic as the son of the son so to speak. And he is an Allen. I just feel so disappointed that I have got absolutely nothing whatsoever from family, either side. Obviously I would have liked it from Dad's side and the only thing that would have been third generation would have been that charm.

Michael made a comment about the watch chain and charm in later years and it was yet another reference to his annoyance with Eileen.

I was livid when I returned on leave to see Eileen wearing the emblem around her neck.

Michael and Penny came home from Oman and he was looking for a job. We had a good friend he wanted to discuss job prospects with. David had been in the Special Investigations Branch in the Army. When he left he got a very good job involving security with a supermarket chain and that was something Michael thought might suit him too.

He asked if I would then set up a meeting with David. I knew Michael was effectively using this contact, and so did David, but he did it for our friendship and met with Michael to discuss various options. However Michael was offered a job as a firearms officer with the Northants Police, which he accepted. That really surprised me because he had never had respect for the Police, perhaps as a result of his interaction with them in his early days as a petty thief?

I distinctly remember him telling me that all policemen were stupid and if they happened to be female that was even worse.

As things turned out, he later had a female Chief Constable as a boss. I believe she was the first in the country, but Michael told me he thought she was 'common'.

~ *Twelve* ~

From the time she was born my father adored Rachel, as did Eileen. She was their only grandchild. My father was quite religious and was keen for Rachel to get confirmed. Rachel went to confirmation classes but was really only doing this for her grandfather. I remember the vicar saying that she was not really ready and I was worried he would not let her go through with it, so I explained it was one of my father's dying wishes.

Unfortunately Dad was far too ill to come to the service, so rather than us having a luncheon afterwards, we drove straight to Milford to see him and Eileen. He was thrilled and his expression of sheer pleasure was wonderful to see. This took place only two or three weeks before he died. I spent a lot of time with him in his final weeks and had an urgent phone call from Eileen a week before his passing telling me 'Dad's time had come'. I dropped everything, left work and because Ian had the car at his work in Trowbridge, got a taxi 50 miles to be with him.

In the week before he passed, on 23rd July 1989, we talked about many things. In particular he regretted being unable to help Ian and I financially as a family as he knew we struggled when we came to England from New Zealand. My father did not think it was right I had to go back to work when Rachel was only five months old but he was in no position to help at that time.

Just before his death he and Eileen gave me a cheque for £50,000. It was his way of making up for what he had been unable to do previously in his life.

It is important to understand that while the cheque was drawn on a Jersey Bank account in Eileen's name, it was my father who signed it. I queried this and they both explained all their joint assets were now in Eileen's name. Obviously my father was not expected to last long, but he still had signing authority on that account.

For me this gift came completely out of the blue and I felt we had to talk about it. So my father, Eileen and I talked about it and I learned the reasons. My father and step-mother wanted us to move house and send Rachel to a private school as they were not happy with her education.

The latter was a sentiment I also shared.

The chat ended with my father saying he knew I would always be there for Eileen and I always was - before my brother put an end to it.

At that time, and to this day, I was in absolutely no doubt what that £50,000 was to be used for. The money was to set Ian, myself and Rachel up in a nice house, as well as assist with Rachel's education. It never occurred to me for one moment that the money they offered was the full extent of their savings. I never discussed their finances with them. That side of things was none of my business.

This letter will provide a view of what my father thought about inheritances. It is dated 1980 and was a condolence letter to us following the death of Ian's father. My father was making reference to the estate of Eileen's aunty at that time-

> How stupid these old people are who hang on to more money than they need and finally it goes to the Government. Are you going to give up work, Adrienne? I hope Rachel is behaving and was glad to know she goes to Sunday School – excellent.

Another letter, written in February 1989 - the year he died - expressed his views on a variety of matters, including his appreciation of the contribution I had made over the years.

> My dear Adrienne, I want you to know what a really happy day you gave me yesterday – the nearest we will ever get to my oft expressed wish for a close-knit family. I do so appreciate all you have contributed (so generously) to the family to keep some semblance of unity in a well nigh impossible situation. You give us both so much, firstly sheer joy and pleasure but so much of your time and effort. To keep a house and home and family also to go to a job is a wonderful effort and does you immense credit. And you still find time to entertain and accommodate us! But you shouldn't spend so much on us. If in any small way I help I am pleased to have the opportunity as any father would. I just wish I had had the chance over the years to do more. Any daughter deserves it from a father but particularly you. Now dear thank you for everything you have done for me and especially the love and kindness you have shown Eileen.

My father clearly loved us, and was a proud and honourable man.

He was also practical and knew he was dying. So everything was put into Eileen's name to save unnecessary costs. He even consulted a funeral director, getting a quote for his services. Sadly, when the account came in, it was more than the quote. Eileen, of course, queried the amount and was unceremoniously informed that it was more to attend a death on a Sunday. Eileen retorted by saying that if my father had known that he would have hung on for another day!

Before he died my father also talked with me about my mother, saying how much he regretted what happened between them. He knew he should never have married her, but it is always easy to be wise with hindsight.

Michael didn't visit our father leading up to his death and this upset me no end. He knew I was extremely upset because he sent me flowers. He had been due to visit that Sunday but on hearing our father had passed away, postponed his trip until the day of the funeral.

I so regret Dad's funeral because it was not how I would have wished it. Eileen asked Dad's old regimental padre to take the service. He lived on the coast not too far away and was only too happy to fill this role, but on the day there was a rail strike or bad weather, something which meant he could not get to us. We were left with no vicar to take the funeral service and a replacement had to step in at the last moment. Eileen wrote a few hurried words about our father's life and gave them to the stand-in vicar. But he obviously knew nothing else about my father. Nowadays, it is the norm for anyone who wishes to say a few words at a funeral to stand up and speak, but not so then.

I felt that my brother should have read a eulogy, or even spoken a few words from the heart, but he didn't. I would have liked to have done so, but was unable to as I was far too upset, as was Eileen.

Many of my father's former army chums were there and I wish they had come back to the house so I could have spoken to them, but none did. Only our family members and close friends were at the wake.

If there is one thing I'm thankful to Eileen for it is that she gave my father the happiest years of his life. It is good to think his life got better after he met Eileen. It would have been very sad indeed if his life had got worse. Eileen also nursed him at home with my help in the last week. She said she would never let him die in hospital, alone, and I am so grateful to her for that.

Eileen made a will in July 1990. It was a year after my father died, so she did not do it in any sort of a rush. She obviously thought long and hard about what she wanted to do at the end of her own life and in that will she left two thirds of her estate to me – bearing in mind her love for our daughter Rachel – and one third to my brother Michael.

She discussed her intentions with me and explained why she was making her will in these specific terms. She also intended leaving pecuniary bequests to her niece, nephew, and the children of her cousin, Ted Farmer, of whom she was extremely fond. It was Eileen's practice to host a party every year on her own birthday and we met Ted and his wife, Janet, and their children on these occasions.

Pecuniary bequests were to be given to two other friends and her brother-in-law and a dinner set was to be left to other friends. In particular she bequeathed a ring to her niece, Dawn.

Eileen's will was prepared by her solicitor, from a local legal firm. At various times later on she discussed her future intentions with me and made it clear she was going to remove Michael as a beneficiary because he never visited her and she felt he didn't care what happened to her. I always persuaded Eileen not to do this, but I phoned Michael on those occasions to tell him he ought to call or visit her. I believe I was successful in urging him to do so.

In June 1999 Eileen added a codicil to her will, drawn up by the same local firm of solicitors, removing one beneficiary because she had not contacted or visited her, but the remainder of her will remained intact, as written.

Almost a year after Dad died, we moved to Canons Close in Warminster, but Rachel clearly didn't want to go to a private school, so we didn't force the issue. The money my father and Eileen gave me was therefore set aside and invested. We had set ourselves up financially and as I worked for a bank we had a favourable mortgage.

During that period I kept a track of how the money gifted to me by my father and Eileen was growing, and continued to let her know, although, of course, there was no obligation for me to do so as it had been given to me for my own use.

At no time did Eileen appear to worry about her own financial situation and by then I was not worrying about our position either. However I knew that if anything happened to me Ian would probably return to New Zealand and Rachel would be leading her own life. So I made a will leaving Eileen £50,000. In due course, these investment funds increased to £70,000 and through a codicil attached to my will I increased the amount which would go to Eileen.

I believe I dealt with the money gifted to me in an extremely fair and honest way. Eileen really lacked for nothing. If she wanted extra money I gave her cash, realising later that this was because she did not want monetary gifts traced.

I learnt later that a few months after my father died, Eileen had a meeting with Social Services and discovered she could claim income support. Showing sums of money in any bank account over a certain limit would disqualify her so she preferred to receive cash.

I know Eileen was pleased about receiving income support, but when I found out I asked her how she could qualify when she had given me £50,000? She just shrugged her shoulders and said she qualified and that was that.

It was suggested much later that my father and Eileen 'set me up' so she could claim income support. I could easily say I believed this to be true, but I don't. Dad was a proud and honourable man. I think Eileen was quite surprised she could claim this type of financial assistance, but it was obvious she did not divulge details of the bank account in Jersey. Had she done so the authorities would have noted the £50,000 withdrawal and would surely have queried it. I know Eileen was also on a disability benefit. She did have problems with her feet or her toes, but she managed to walk quite well. One day one of her friends took me aside and told me she knew Eileen was on disability and should take great care not to be seen striding along the cliffs without her walking stick. I relayed this to Eileen when we next talked and she was more careful after that.

I know my father and Eileen did not want Michael to know about the money I was given so I promised not to divulge it. After Dad died, Eileen did discuss adding me as a co-signatory to her bank account, but I was not keen on the idea, and didn't push it. I eventually forgot all about the joint account idea and Eileen never proposed it again. I also forgot about a draft letter Eileen asked me to write which was to make its appearance many years later.

During 1990 we moved into our new home in Canons Close and it wasn't long before I was experiencing my second brush with the Courts. All fourteen houses in the Close were approached by a driveway and this was bordered on one side by lovely flowering shrubs. It looked very attractive but soon after we moved in the Close was 'adopted' by the local Council and I heard that the intention was to rip out the shrubs and lay grass in their place. The reason given by the council was that the shrubs were planted over the service strip and if maintenance was required, it would be 'too difficult' with the shrubs there.

I was none too pleased at the proposal and nor were the neighbours. We asked the council officials why they could not just take the shrubs out when and if required?

We felt that removing the shrubs permanently would have a detrimental effect on the attractiveness of the road and the market value of the houses. After all that's why we bought all our houses. It was a massive selling point.

Councils being councils, the officials stuck to their plan, despite many letters and complaints from neighbours, headed by myself. Personally I thought our case should be against the builders who should have known the shrubs were over the service strip and should not have been planted there in the first place. But we found out that the planning approvals were at issue, therefore the fault lay with the council. Permission should not have been given in the first place.

I took the council to Court, but lost. It was an open and shut case really as I didn't own the land. The council fortunately didn't ask for costs but the Magistrate tore a strip off my solicitors because they should have advised me I had no case. Needless to say, the solicitors put their hand out for their not inconsiderable fees, despite me losing in Court.

That said, I had made a point. The story was well covered in the local newspapers and I hope lessons were learned as the council was then forced to compromise. This taught me a valuable lesson – that while one battle may be lost, no-one should assume the war is finally over. It should also have taught me another lesson – never trust solicitors!

Having removed the shrubs, the council did little to maintain the grass, which ended up being overgrown and unruly. Eventually, at our suggestion, more suitable shrubs were planted and the neighbours agreed to look after them.

One positive outcome of the neighbourhood working party was that we made great friends with Bob and Dorothy, who lived in the house at the top of the drive. They would arrive with drinks for the workers and it really ended up being quite fun. Dorothy is still a great friend although Bob has passed away. I believe to this day the neighbours still occasionally carry out work party duties on 'the strip' to keep it tidy.

Having moved to Canons Close that year we were not going to have a holiday, but our lovely cousins, Nic and Jen, made an offer we couldn't refuse. They had a timeshare unit in The Gambia, West Africa, and offered to let us use it for a week. All we had to pay was the airfare and, of course, our expenses while we were there. It was not the time to visit The Gambia, being the middle of the summer, but we did. It proved to be both the best and the worst holiday of our lives! The timeshare was beautifully set on a lovely beach but the weather was very hot and sticky.

The town of Banjul, nearby, was the pits, but it did provide some experiences. One of them we did not enjoy – all of us became ill. I had never been ill on holiday before and Ian was very sick on the way home. However we met the locals, who were beautiful people. I could have sold Rachel many times over for a few head of cattle! The head of the market traders met us on the beach one day and invited Rachel and I to join his family for a picnic. Rachel dropped an item of food on the sand and was going to pick it up and eat it, but the trader took it from her and gave it to one of his own children to eat!

One evening Rachel decided to sit outside late, but about one o'clock in the morning I realised she was not in bed and went down to look for her. She was on the patio, cornered by a very large crab flexing its pincers at her. She didn't want to yell out for fear of waking people. We had been told not to walk the beach at night and now we saw why. It was swarming with crabs. You could have walked to the sea on their backs and not touched the sand.

I have noted recently on a map of Banjul that there is a zone called the Crab Island ponding area. It is little wonder that so many crabs invade the beach in that locality but it was a certainly a sight to behold with so many of those creatures keeping company with each other on that visit.

Another day when we went down to the beach it was swarming with heavily-armed soldiers. Talks were being held between Liberian and Sierra Leone leaders over the civil war at the time, so the area was literally heaving with security.

The day before we left The Gambia we went on a riverboat cruise and I am sure it was on that excursion Ian got food poisoning. Rachel and I had already succumbed and had recovered by then.

On departure day I remember the airport being crowded with people. It was free-for-all boarding the plane as no seats had been allocated and it was well overbooked. The airline people were asking passengers to volunteer to be 'bumped' but no one wanted to. Usually we would have jumped at the chance of a few extra days on holiday but on this occasion we literally ran for the plane and fortunately got on before other intending travellers!

The British Airways crew on this flight had been on our river trip and the pilot had said if we sent him a message while in flight he would invite us into the cockpit, which he did. He told us the crew had been sick also, with one of the hostesses so ill she could not return to England on our flight and had to stay in Banjul another week.

Nic and Jen were really good friends, as well as cousins. They had a large beautiful house near Salisbury and would host big family luncheon parties and evening parties. We would seldom go to the evening parties because we had Rachel, and it was too far, but we went to lunch many times and vice versa. They would usually end up hosting everyone on Easter Sunday.

Nic's sisters and their children and his mother, Judy, would sometimes be there, as would my mother and Bill, and Jenny would cook a huge goose or turkey. Rachel was faddy about food in those days but Jenny would always manage to put on fish fingers for her.

One day the kitchen door was left open and the carcass of a consumed goose was left on the table. Nic and Jen had two Irish setters and my brother had a Great Dane. So, of course, there the three dogs were with the carcass on the floor, and grease everywhere. Jenny simply laughed.

Michael's wife Penny did not like Nic and Jen - or indeed any of his immediate family - but she did show some fondness towards them now and then when it served her purpose.

In another one of his audio tapes, Michael demonstrated this:-

The barbecue with Nic and Jen, Penny hasn't mentioned a word about it. I suppose she still has her thing on about Jenny, which is now getting to the point of being ridiculous considering how much Jenny has done for us. Well, I'll have that out with Penny when I get home. No, I mean Penny has written very frequently with all the news, etc. but no mention that Nic and Jen had turned up with half the stuff we had left. I don't know whether Penny had spoken to Jenny at all and had got the right side but I know there was an agreement that we were going to give some of the stuff to her. Anyway, I will sort that out with my wife when I see her next.

That is not to say Michael and Penny were not wonderful hosts themselves. We would go up and stay at the Windmill, taking walks along the canal bank or into the country. They were generous with their gifts too, although not always successfully. We had a laugh once about a pasta-maker they gave me, the point being everyone knew I was a hopeless cook. But the interesting one was a book called Colour Me Beautiful. This had just been released as ladies were beginning to 'look at their colours' and only wear those that suited them. I had never heard of it at that time.

I thanked Penny for the book as it looked interesting. Penny recounted that she had been at work and a workmate came in looking absolutely marvellous. She went on then to explain that this woman was usually a mousy-looking person with no sense of style, but she had had her colours done. 'I immediately thought of you,' Penny quipped.

My brother told me about the difficulties he had with Penny not being keen on any of his family. She certainly did not like our father or Eileen. But Michael said he had told her his relationship with me was non-negotiable and that we would continue to go and stay - and she would make us all welcome. She was under his orders and certainly made an effort for us, producing lovely meals. However, I remember one occasion when we were invited for lunch as we were staying in the district at the time. I thought it would only a case of popping in to have lunch with my brother and sister-in-law, but when we arrived there was another couple there and instead it was a smart, dressed up affair. We had Rachel with us and Penny greeted us curtly by saying she had not been expecting all of us, with the inference being that she had not expected our daughter to be with us. To me it was reminiscent of her earlier outburst when Dad, Eileen, Ted and Janet arrived at the Windmill for coffee one day.

As it turned out Penny had only six pork chops for the meal and there was not enough for Rachel. So she was thrown a bag of potato crisps and told to eat them in the kitchen - in case she made a mess! Rachel has never forgotten that. If anybody had turned up unexpectedly at our house, I would have cut a pork chop in two and given half each to Ian and myself, whispering FHB - family hold back.

The weekends with my brother and his wife could be embarrassing. We would often go for walks, with Michael and Ian striding ahead and I would be left with Penny. All she would do was talk about my brother - and not in a very complimentary way – with their sex life, or rather lack of it, being top of the agenda. She also told me that if she had somewhere else to go she would leave Michael. I did not want to listen to this and would ask Ian not to leave me with her on the walks. Penny also regretted not having children, with the fault lying with my brother, she insisted. She always felt he knew he was sterile maintaining he should have told her this before they got married.

Another confidentiality Penny shared with me was the fact that she had her name included on the deeds of her mother's house. I am not sure how this came into the conversation but I do remember at the time thinking it was a wise move and one which her brother might not have approved of, as, of course, it would consequently mean the house would go directly to Penny on her mother's death.

Their marriage was a strange one. On one occasion my brother told me all about his Army pension and said that if anything happened to him this would go to me. I was quite astounded, saying that his pension would surely go to his widow. But no, he insisted, he was permitted to nominate anyone – and he had nominated me.

Once we had a holiday with Michael and Penny in America. We were going to take Rachel to Disney World and they decided to come too. It didn't go too badly because we arranged not to stick rigidly together, but to do our own thing if we wanted. One day they offered to look after Rachel so Ian and I could have some time alone. Rachel said afterwards it wasn't much fun because she wanted to play board games, but Penny wouldn't participate. So Penny sulked and went off to read a book while Michael played the games with Rachel.

On another day Michael and Ian looked after Rachel while Penny and I went on a day cruise to Grand Bahama. I knew as long as I did what Penny wanted it would be fine. The choice for shore excursions was to the beach, the shops, or the botanical gardens. Out of all the passengers only eight wanted to visit the Botanical Gardens so the ship arranged a taxi to take us there. However when the driver suggested the beach or the town Penny said in no uncertain terms that we were going to the botanical gardens. So we did. On arrival the driver said he would wait for ten minutes, which he claimed would be more than enough time to view these particular botanical gardens. He was right – there was nothing at all interesting to see. So the taxi driver took us to the beach and the town, giving us a really good tour. So good was the tour that we arrived back at the ship's side with only five minutes to spare before sailing.

I had another similar experience on a trip with Penny. This trip was supposed to involve orange groves but Penny soon realised we were going to miss them and she complained very loudly on the bus. The driver advised we would not be going to orange groves and there was a big argument over the matter. The driver sought to end the debate by asking the rest of us if we wanted to see orange groves. No-one put their hand up except Penny, until she then dug me in the ribs, in effect forcing me to put my hand up too. It was noticeable Michael did not support her. Out-voted by an overwhelming majority, we did not get to see the orange groves!

While on the subject of holidays abroad, one other occasion Michael and Penny went to one of the Caribbean Islands with another couple. The plane was late landing in Miami and they got held up at Customs. Timing was tight for the connecting flight, so Penny said she would go ahead to 'hold the flight'. Michael told me later he told her not to, thinking at least if they all missed it, they would all still be together. But Penny did not listen and left the other three. It appears she got lost because Michael and his friends caught the flight, but Penny did not. I often wondered what husband would get on a flight without his wife? The answer was Michael. They were both in a mood the whole holiday as a result and I am so glad that we were nowhere near them during this particular excursion.

~ Thirteen ~

After my father died, Eileen and I had an excellent relationship for 10 years. She came to stay and Ian, Rachel and I often visited her also. Dad and Eileen loved car boot sales and made quite a thing of it together, buying and selling for some profit. I used to help her, either near her home or at sales near Warminster. We had a lot of fun together doing this.

Eileen came to us every other Christmas and in the alternate year went to her cousin, Ted Farmer. She never spent Christmas with Michael and Penny and certainly did not go on holiday with them. As far as I can remember, she only went to stay with them once. We had five holidays abroad together and on one occasion I went with her to Teneriffe, where she had friends.

We made great friends with our American neighbour in Canons Close. His name was John and he was going to settle in the United Kingdom with his wife. They came over to look at properties but tragically his wife was killed in a car accident. John continued with his plan to reside in Britain and bought a house across the road from us. He was a real gadget man and installed a satellite dish in his back garden about two metres across so he could pick up television stations from all over the world. He was the first person we knew to get a digital camera. We have it now and I am sure it is a museum piece! He was also the first person we knew to get satellite navigation in his car, which impressed my brother immensely.

John became a big part of our family and we started to include him on visits to Eileen. He always came over to our house if she was visiting us and would help us with Eileen's car boot sales. His Jaguar was much bigger than our car.

On one holiday Ian and I flew over to France to stay with some friends in their country cottage. When they returned home to Warminster we stayed on and John drove Eileen over to join us, taking the car on the ferry. They had a good trip and we all thoroughly enjoyed ourselves.

John owned a travel agency in the United States, a sleeping partner not active in the business. However he got many good deals and was invited to take his car through the Channel tunnel when it first opened in 1994. This first trip by the general public was by invitation only and Ian and I went along with John.

Then the four of us – John, Eileen, Ian and I – went over to the Christmas markets in Germany. We flew to Strasbourg and John hired a car there. He had booked us into nice hotels in Strasbourg and Nuremberg and once again we had a wonderful time. It was all so beautiful and John knew exactly where to go.

Eileen then met Douggie, who was one of her neighbours, living in the same block of apartments as her, and they struck up a friendship. We welcomed Douggie into our family also and he was included in our Christmas celebrations. We took him and Eileen twice abroad on holiday, including a trip to Austria, where we stayed in Kitzbühel for two weeks. Douggie captured a lot of it on video camera which we still have and everyone's excitement and enjoyment of the trip is there for all to see. Ian took Douggie on his first chairlift ride up a mountain. He was about eighty six at the time. Eileen would not have managed to get on, so I stayed below with her as the men went up.

We looked after Eileen and Douggie well on that trip, but there was an embarrassing moment when it was time for us to all leave to return to the United Kingdom. On this day we were told the bus could not get right to the hotel because Kitzbühel – a small medieval town - had narrow streets. We would therefore have to get aboard quickly as the bus would be blocking the road. The four of us were outside the hotel with our luggage when the bus stopped up the street and the driver called and told us to get on as quickly as we could. With that Douggie and Eileen ran for it, leaving Ian and I to carry their luggage, as well as our own. We were fortunate the courier came to our rescue.

We also took Eileen and Douggie to Lake Como in Italy. On this occasion we had booked a holiday with our friends, Rose and David, but Eileen expressed an interest and so we obliged by taking them also. Again, they needed a lot of assistance and care, as Douggie in particular got totally confused with the currency, which was the Italian Lira in those days. He frequently handed over ten million lira when he needed to pay only one million, so we had to keep a close watch on what he was doing the whole time.

There was one incident however which left me unhappy with Eileen. It occurred while Ian was away on a trip back to New Zealand. I had gone to stay with Eileen and together with Douggie we all went out to lunch. It was a new restaurant they had found which they liked but as things turned out the meal was not good and the service was poor that day. But I paid for our meals as a treat. Eileen told me later she had phoned the restaurant to complain about the meal and service and she and Douggie were offered a free meal as compensation!

I thought that was a bit naughty of Eileen as I had paid for the meals. So I phoned the restaurant and Ian and I were then offered free meals too. He had just got back from New Zealand and imagine the surprise for Douggie and Eileen when we arrived the same day at the same time for the freebie! I did not expect the wine to be included with the free meal, but Eileen did. She and Douggie then walked out of the restaurant, leaving me to pay for the wine. Ian and I just laughed as we had a nice meal and everyone had enjoyed themselves.

On other occasions I found Eileen could be a trifle dishonest. She once booked a trip to South Africa, saying she would go with a cousin, but she later realised it really was beyond her capabilities. So she went to a doctor and obtained a medical certificate, then asked me to arrange to get the money back through her insurance.

At one stage Eileen wanted to change her car and we talked her out of that as her existing vehicle was perfectly adequate for what she needed. At times she was also pretty extravagant. When my father was alive, for example, she went out and bought a mink coat. Dad thought it was absolutely ridiculous for the money, so she took it back.

Just as we had welcomed Douggie into our home, so did we make an effort for Eileen's friends and for her niece and family. They would often come for lunch and stay the rest of day. Some of her friends even came to stay for weekends while Douggie and Eileen were with us. We had a great relationship with them all.

My brother and his wife Penny were not so endeared to Eileen and often revealed they did not like her. They thought she was common but I always tried to keep the peace. Eileen knew what they thought of her, but she was actually quite proud of my brother for reasons best known to her. Michael would attend Eileen's birthday parties and I often felt she was showing him off to those who attended. We always attended too, but Penny would not.

A silhouette photo of Michael appears on the front cover of a book by Tony Geraghty called This is the SAS and Eileen had that book standing up proudly on the mantelpiece for all to see. My brother was quite scathing in his opinion of people who wrote books on the SAS insisting they were 'cashing in on the Regiment.' He later mentioned the SAS book to Rachel, saying it annoyed him that Eileen had it on the mantle-shelf. That was 'so naff', he told my daughter. In later years Eileen would take the book down when Michael visited but Douggie said she then put it right it back immediately he had gone. There were no other pictures on that mantelpiece, apart from a small one of my father. As for Ian, Rachel and I, we didn't exist, in photographic terms at least.

~ *Fourteen* ~

Our American neighbour John remained a very dear friend to the end of his days. He was included in many parties, lunches, dinners, holidays and in the outings we had with Eileen, and then with Douggie after he came on the scene. Eileen simply loved men. She liked their company and was certainly not the sort of person to have a coffee or lunch with the girls. She liked John's company, and particularly liked to believe that both Douggie and John craved her attention. That may have been the case with Douggie, but I know to John she was just my step-mother and part of the family.

Whenever John was lonely he would wander across the road to our house. If we were watching television, he would join us. If I was cooking dinner, he would sit in the kitchen and talk. At times he would wander over with a large pot in his hands saying he had made dinner. It was usually Mexican, or a goulash and we would all sit and enjoy it together. It was a cherished relationship for us all.

Being very much the gadget man John would always be buying something in that style. Once he bought an ice-cream maker and only used it once. He then bought a three-tier steamer and left it at our house so we could work out how to use it. Once while in Sydney he bought a telescope but he then left it with Ian, again to see how it worked. It was top of the range and would automatically find planets and stars, but it did take Ian quite a while to fathom as the barrel kept pointing itself below the horizon. Ian eventually ascertained that it had been set for the southern skies and was automatically finding the southern hemisphere. Once Ian got it set it up for the northern hemisphere all worked to plan, but again John wanted to leave it at our house. It was just another gadget he really had no use for.

John loved taking his Jaguar over to the Continent and particularly enjoyed driving it through the Eastern European countries. He knew his way around those places and would usually come home with the bumper almost touching the road as the Jag would be so heavily laden with beer samples from different countries for Ian – and a few bottles of wines for me, although he was not a drinker himself.

John had one half-brother called Mike and he came over from America on a couple of occasions. He lived in a trailer van in New Mexico, in a place called Truth and Consequences. Mike was a real character but entirely different to John. At times they argued and on one occasion Mike left for home without telling John, simply phoning from the airport to say goodbye.

We met John's business partner in the travel agency, Susan, who visited with her husband George. We met his other American friends also and often entertained them at our house. John adored Rachel and he felt close enough to discuss his will, even asking me to be an executor. I agreed but I understood he did not actually have a will, so I told him he should go to local solicitors who were offering free advice on such matters. John made an appointment but I think it was going to cost him £10 to have a will drawn up so he didn't bother to go back.

John came to New Zealand with us twice on holiday and we showed him a lot of that country. When we finally settled in New Zealand for good, he came twice more and stayed with us. On his last trip he was not particularly well and could not walk very far, but he loved sitting in a chair in the sun, playing with the latest gadget he had bought. I can see him now in my mind, and can remember thinking he didn't look to be in good health. I doubted he got around to making that will, but I said nothing.

On his trip back to the United Kingdom he went via the United States, as he usually did, so he could see Susan and George and then his half-brother. He left New Zealand but never made it back to the United Kingdom alive. He suffered a stroke on the plane, never regaining consciousness and after lingering a few days in a Chicago hospital he died. Susan subsequently spoke to the air hostess who had attempted to revive him and she said he was such a lovely man. She said he told her about the lovely holiday he just had in New Zealand, meeting up with us, then his friends in Sacramento, and his half-brother. His death was very sad to us, but he died doing what he loved most, travelling.

We learned that John had not made a will. He died intestate so his half-brother Mike went to England and sold off almost everything, although he did give some things to John's friends and neighbours. He gave us the telescope and friends brought it to New Zealand for us but it was actually damaged in transit and never worked again. Such is life. John's half-brother was certainly not a rich man, until then, and it is right that he should have inherited. I am sure – and certainly hope – he is enjoying the money.

It was around 1993 when we learned my cousin, Nic and his wife, Jen, were having deep problems with their marriage. We were about to go over to lunch one day for his birthday, but Jen phoned to say he had taken off and disappeared. We had never suspected anything was wrong, but things really went from bad to worse, much to our disappointment.

Nic eventually moved out and, the divorce proceedings were horrendous. Both of them were well off in their own right with Nic being a dentist in Romsey, Hampshire, and Jenny owned a property relocation business in Southampton and many investment properties. You would have thought it would have been easy for them as a couple, but that was not so and they fought tooth and nail for every solitary penny. Naturally it was the solicitors who won in the end.

In these circumstances it was difficult to be a friend to both. I listened and tried to advise them to sort things out amicably and Michael agreed also that this should be their objective.

Nic had to move from their lovely home into a flat and he continued his drinking late into the night, sometimes phoning me at some unearthly hour. I would advise him to look to the future and think that in five years' time the dust would be settled and he would be in his own property somewhere.

It came as a big disappointment when Jenny informed us she was going to build a new life and would therefore be breaking all ties, certainly with everyone in Nic's family and she did. But many years later I discovered she is still in contact with my brother.

All the children, including Rachel loved Jenny and the strange thing is we are not really in contact with Nic either these days.

Jenny was wonderful with children, but Nic could not give her any. Jen told me Nic had insinuated he had not loved her for quite a long time and I suppose I can understand her anger when she lamented that if he had told her that years beforehand they could have divorced then and perhaps she would have met someone who could have given her children.

I often wonder how Jen felt when Nic subsequently married the dental nurse who worked for him. She had four children and Nic is now a proud step-grandfather. His new family kept him really busy but the relationship he had with the younger daughter, Holly was always a real struggle. At one time she accused him of molesting her, there was a screaming match and she threatened to call the Police, but nothing ever came of it. It was another case of the anguish people suffer when accused of something they perhaps did not do.

~ *Fifteen* ~

Rachel left school and went to a secretarial college in London, taking computer skills and business studies, but after two terms she left as she said she knew everything she needed to know in order to get a job. She opted to stay in London, securing a position and moving into a flat with one of her colleagues from the college.

In 1995 Michael then suggested Rachel move into his investment flat in Fulham. It suited him and by then Rachel was looking to change flatmates and needed somewhere else to live. Michael worked out her rental to the last penny. He also worked out what he would save by not needing an agent to look after the place and how much tax he would save too by saying his niece was living there rent free. That was not true of course but it demonstrates how calculating he can really be when he involves unwitting, naïve people in his money-making schemes.

Ian went in and painted the flat and we arranged to have a new shower put in, although Michael paid for it. Ian had to go to the flat and waited while the workers installed it as Rachel and her flatmate were out all day at work.

However when Michael said it would be convenient for Rachel to have the flat because any time he and Penny were in London he would have somewhere to stay, we really did put our foot down. We knew that would not work and it certainly would not be fair on Rachel or her flatmate as they were paying the rental. Besides, I had memories of Michael running his finger over the tops of the doors looking for dust when we rented his Durrington property.

Having spent a year in Michael's flat Rachel moved to Australia in 1996. We bought her a one way ticket for her 21st birthday and she has remained there ever since, making occasional trips home to England.

During one of those trips home, we got a call that Mother had suffered a heart attack. She was rushed to hospital, and William - as we had started to call Bill – was placed temporarily into a nursing home as he suffered badly from multiple sclerosis and could not manage by himself. Both my brother and I went to Bridlington and stayed in their house. Mother was very sick and her health could have gone either way.

I clearly remember my brother briefing me, saying he would 'handle everything' to do with our mother. He intended speaking to the doctor to find out just what was happening and he emphasised again that I was to leave things in his hands. But, as soon as we were confronted with a doctor whose accent was so strong neither of us could understand a word, my brother formed an entirely different view, telling me I could speak to the doctor in future.

Michael and I stayed in Mother's house together and while rummaging, he found her will. He was horrified to see that Mother had left Iain Bryce, a 'family friend', one of the best grandfather clocks. Michael declared he would put a stop to that. It was like history revisiting itself – Mother too had been horrified in the past, because my grandmother had given her family doctor one of her impressive clocks. It is with the doctor's family to this day.

I do not have an Allens' grandfather clock. My brother had one and he later told me Mother gave him to it. Actually he had asked for it as he thought it would be suited to the Windmill. He felt he should let me know in case I was upset, or had strong feelings about it. I was indeed very upset as I had never been offered any of the Allens' clocks, but I said nothing.

After a couple of days in Mother's house, my brother decided there was nothing more he could do so he went home, saying he was required back at work. His logic was that his work was more important than mine. It was just before Christmas 1998 and Mother's house was bitterly cold. It was one of those old large semis with windows in the bedrooms that iced up on the inside overnight. My mother didn't have decent heating but she was worried about getting Christmas cards and gifts delivered. Michael was adamant he would not be staying on to deliver Christmas presents for her, so I did.

Mother did recover and eventually returned home. Michael then suggested that she should execute an enduring power of attorney and this was duly prepared, with Michael and I both being appointed to the role. I mention this here because it is another example that the dissent between my mother and I was well and truly behind us and that she trusted me completely.

Not long after this Michael and Penny moved from the Windmill to a house in Pattishall which was very nice, large, and modern. He had found the Windmill a lot of work as our father had foreseen and he also told me that Penny was not liked in the village. She made enemies easily, he revealed, so they decided on a fresh start in Pattishall.

Michael invited Eileen and Douggie to stay for a spell at the new house and although she wasn't keen on going, I persuaded her to, saying my brother was making some effort. They did stay for a short while, but the visit was not a success as both parties later admitted. Michael said they had gone to a nice restaurant for dinner but Eileen embarrassed them deeply by 'actually engaging the waiter in conversation'.

Eileen also had a habit of putting her uneaten food on other people's plates, hoping they would finish it. We were used to that, but Michael was appalled. 'She put food on my plate', he exclaimed, in somewhat of a checked rage.

While on that visit Eileen wanted to take a photograph of the house, but before she was out of earshot she overheard Penny complaining to Michael. Her 'crime' it seems was that her photograph would be of the house, not those who lived in it!

In 1999, our old friend Mike – the father of my god-daughter Debbie - asked Ian if he was going to be making a trip to New Zealand as he would like to join him. Mike was a widower as his wife Jane had died a few years previously. Ian had not planned to travel so far that year as I was hoping to get redundancy from the bank and we thought we would do a big trip together the following year. But Ian agreed to show Mike around New Zealand, saying it would be cost effective as the car and accommodation would be shared. They had a great time and Mike fell in love with New Zealand. That trip meant a lot to him, as was to be seen later.

~ *Sixteen* ~

Times were changing drastically at the bank by then and managers no longer had secretaries. Computers had arrived and managers were then expected to type all their own reports. My duties changed accordingly and I was assigned to sending out standard overdraft notices, and selling, selling, selling. I hated selling – it was not something I joined the bank to do – but I certainly did not want to become a cashier either. From the moment computers were installed, we were expected to turn our hand to anything.

Fortunately, I had an extremely good relationship with my manager and he stuck by me. I suggested if I was not to be a secretary any more, then the bank could consider making me redundant. In effect in a major restructure everyone was expected to apply for their own jobs, but my job no longer existed. I asked what would happen if I did not apply for any job and I was told that by law I could be forced to take any job – anywhere. That could even be in Trowbridge, or Bath, some considerable distance away, with travel required each day. But for as long as I had been at the bank, my walk to work had been just seven minutes!

With my future uncertain, and a loathing for the prospect of more selling or being a cashier, I crossed my fingers and hoped for the best. Someone higher up was on my side as I managed to obtain one of the last packages the bank was offering. Being 51, I qualified for a pension immediately and received a lump sum pay-out as well.

It was August 1999 and then it happened! I will always remember the circumstances, and the repercussions haunt me every day. It was my last contracted day at work, and my birthday. Ian and I travelled down and spent the weekend at Eileen's. We had a wonderful time and while there discussed the idea of taking her and Douggie to New Zealand for a trip since they always wanted to go.

Douggie also talked about taking Eileen on a cruise around the Scottish Isles for her eightieth birthday, but she took me to one side, saying she was worried. Douggie would be paying for the trip and they were both well aware that it would be cheaper to have a double cabin than two singles. This was an issue for Eileen and had always been a bit of a bone of contention between them during trips abroad, as their relationship was absolutely platonic.

Knowing this was of concern to my step-mother, I had a quiet word with Douggie, telling him she was quite worried about the prospect of taking a double cabin. He was absolutely adamant he would never do anything she didn't want to do. So separate sleeping accommodation it would be, as usual. Eileen was thrilled I had settled that, throwing her arms around me and thanking me for easing her worries.

We left Eileen and Douggie in the best of spirits, or so it seemed. That evening I phoned to thank Eileen for such a wonderful weekend. We had all had such a lovely time and I was feeling great, as was Ian.

I just could not believe what followed and to this day wonder how things could have gone so horribly wrong in such a short space of time. I could tell immediately from Eileen's tone that she was angry about something – very angry. 'I don't know how you have the audacity to discuss my sleeping arrangements with Douggie,' she shouted down the phone.

I was really taken aback and completely astounded at this verbal attack coming out of the blue, but I kept calm saying she should think about what she had said and phone me back later. With that I put the phone down, possibly a little too sharply.

I discussed what had happened with Ian and he advised me to leave it and Eileen would phone back. But she didn't and if there was ever a point in time you wished you could go back to, that was it.

I now know I should have phoned her to settle it there and then, but I didn't. I concluded it was up to her to contact me to apologise – but she never did.

Later I phoned my brother to tell him what had happened. He just laughed. But then Eileen phoned him and told him all sorts of weird and wonderful stories about me stealing her money and not giving it back. So from mole hills hefty mountains do grow.

Surprisingly – or perhaps not surprisingly as things have turned out – Michael got involved and took Eileen's side with some ease, although there was no evidence I had done what I was being accused of and I can say, hand on Bible, that I never stole anything from my step-mother. Indeed the accusation that I did has never been put in writing.

Michael and I had meetings and discussions about the situation and I remember Ian telling me this would split up my brother and I, something I did not accept would happen. But Ian is a very astute man, and what he predicted came to pass.

The loving sibling relationship came to an abrupt end during a telephone conversation. When I declared I would not be writing a cheque for Eileen for the £50,000 everything changed in an instant. Michael's manner changed abruptly and he snarled threateningly: 'Then on your fucking head be it!', slamming the phone down. That was the day my brother declared war – on me!

I have to say that while this particularly nasty choice of words unsettled me somewhat that day, I didn't think much of it because I believed the molehill of a rift created by Eileen would be sorted amicably when the dust settled. However, it was about that time I began to have restless nights and I often dreamed of this silly episode. It is also when I began to fear my brother and his SAS training.

1. My brother, Michael and I - a picture of innocence

2. Michael and I. We were good friends until the issue of inheritances came between us.

3. My Granny and G'pa Lobb. I never saw my grandfather dressed any differently. He always had a high starched collar and heirloom watch and chain.

4. My last day at Bridlington High School for Girls. I am the fourth from left and Oggy is fifth from left.

5. Happy days at the beach bungalow. (From left) Michael, Mother, Sally and Aunty Ruth.

6. Dog walking days. Sally (on left) and Oggy.

7. Sheila and I climbing Ayers Rock in Australia in 1971.

8. My father, Maurice Lobb, and my brother Michael.

9. The four generations at Rachel's Christening in September 1975 – me, Mother and my grandmother Allen with Rachel.

10. The same family members when Rachel was nine years old.

11. At Mother's house in St James Road, Bridlington. (From left) My cousin Madeleine, Rachel, Uncle Trevor and Mother.

12. My father and Eileen with Rachel at their home.

13 and 14: Rachel with her Uncle Michael, whom she adored and was always pleased to see.

15. My Mother.

16. Michael and Penny at our house before a formal dinner function.

17. Michael and Penny

18. Michael and Penny's salubrious home, The Windmill, Napton-on-the-Hills, Warwickshire, England.

19. Our more modest abode, at 66 Sambourne Gardens in Warminster.

20. My cousin Nic and his wife
   Jenny.

21. Our good friend and
   neighbour, John Dimidowich.

22. Rachel with her grandpa
   William and grandmother
   during a Christmas visit to
   the United Kingdom from
   Australia.

23. Eileen and Douggie at an
   outdoor concert at Longleat,
   one of the many outings we
   enjoyed together. Events like
   this were common.

24. Eileen with Rachel at her 18th birthday celebration in 1962. Eileen was integrated into our family and often joined us for such events.

25. Mother's sister, Aunty Ruth.

26. Rachel and Jamie at their wedding in November 2007. (From left) Jamie's mother June, Jamie and Rachel, Ian and I, and good friends Mike and Brenda Hughes.

27. Christmas 2010 – Ian and I with Rachel, Jamie and their first son Evan.

28. Ian with his children. (From left) Pam, Linda and Rob.

29. Our grandson Evan and I at a picnic table on the shores of Lake Taupo, Central North Island, New Zealand. Ian and I gifted this table to our town in memory of our fathers, Ian Matthewson Nairn and Maurice Lobb.

30. Evan's birthday in May 2012 with his new brother Curtis, Rachel and Jamie.

Part Two

~ *Seventeen* ~

I had known my father was in dispute with glaziers over repairs to the leaking patio doors in the penthouse apartment at the time of his death. It appears they had not done a good job and therefore he would not pay them, preparing instead to let the Court decide the matter.

Following his passing, the glaziers demanded my step-mother settle the bill. It appears Eileen told my brother about the demand, but she did not tell me. Michael paid the bill without question and without my knowledge. If he had discussed the matter with me I would have advised him Dad was disputing the workmanship. Indeed, as my father predicted, the windows still leaked and more work had to be carried out at a later date.

Eileen told me about it a few years later – before our big argument. I was concerned, asking if she thought it was fair to let my brother pay when she had given me the £50,000. But she just shrugged her shoulders so I let it go.

After the dispute with Eileen, Michael raised this matter, so I paid my brother £3422.16 to cover the work. The cheque he cashed, dated 25th November 1999 is now in my possession. At the time I asked for a receipt for the work carried out by the glaziers, but I have never received it to this day

Later Michael gave me another invoice, dated 30th August 2000, for £1864. This was for more work on the windows at the apartment, which he expected me to pay. But I refused to do so because he still had not produced a receipt for the previous work.

I must state here that the money for the glazing was not all I had paid out following my father's death in 1989. Whenever Eileen needed money, I gave her what she wanted as I had promised my father I would look after her and I continued to honour that pledge in the ten years until we fell out so rapidly and dramatically.

Michael responded to my refusal to pay the bill for the latest work to the apartment, advising me curtly, by letter:-

There is no point in asking for receipts retrospectively – any more than you were prepared to provide receipts or make any account for the money whatsoever over the last ten years – or substantiate that you did not steal the money.

This was, of course, a reference to the fact that Eileen and Michael were accusing me of stealing the £50,000. If that was the case – I deny emphatically that I did so - I wonder why neither reported it to the police. It was, after all, a substantial amount of money in 1989, and even today.

I have often asked myself why my step-mother, guided by my brother, did not take such an obvious step. If they were so certain of their grounds, they would surely have done so, as there was a significant financial incentive for them.

At one stage Ian and I went to Eileen's to try and find an amicable solution to our difficulties. I pointed out to Eileen that if she had really considered the monetary gift to me rightfully belonged to her she should never have claimed income support. With that amount of money on hand, or invested, she would have been guilty of committing social security fraud and that is something I would never have acceded to.

While with Eileen that day – Douggie was a witness to all that transpired – I discussed my father's autobiography, dedicated to Rachel. This had been in my possession and as a retirement project I intended transcribing it. Eileen decided she wanted it back to read it again, so at one of our meetings I had returned it.

On this last visit, Ian and I believed we were making headway. Things between Eileen and I were a little frosty, but we parted almost friends again. Eileen offered me the autobiography back but when she stated she still wanted to re-read it, I suggested I would leave it with her until she had. This turned out to be a mistake – it took years, and a Court case, to retrieve it. However I left that meeting believing we could get our once-close relationship back on track. Although I did not know it at that time however, this was something my brother was definitely not going to allow. I had always known that once he embarked on any mission whatsoever, he would not relent in any way. Eventually, matters deteriorated even more.

The battle within our family intensified through what I believe was a vicious, vindictive campaign against me by my brother. It was a scary prospect because I knew no-one would want to cross him in any way. We were dealing with a man who, by his own admission years earlier, thought nothing of killing. To Michael, it was a job, no more, no less.

Michael was an ex-SAS soldier, one who was used to working in the shadows. He was trained in such techniques and by all accounts, he was good at it. One example of this involved a phone call to the bank I used to work for. During this call he made an appointment to see the manager - in the name of the Northants Police – but he also stated he had concerns about me. Just before the due date he cancelled that appointment. I should not have ever learned about this incident, given the banking regulations, but one of my former colleagues told me about it. I wondered what Michael was up to, but I thought no more of it.

Having decided a face-to-face meeting with bank officials was not in his best interests, my brother then phoned the bank's assistant manager, aware that a telephone conversation could not, in any way, be used against him. This call purported to be a 'discussion', but when the assistant manager realised what my brother was really saying, he terminated the conversation, rightly so. Discussing matters involving members of staff with third parties was strictly forbidden in banking terms, as it is in most businesses.

It was after I learned of the developments in Michael's on-going campaign against me that my dreams intensified, starting to cause me even greater concern.

On 30th December 1999 my stepmother wrote me a letter. As with many of those later sent by her, it was typed, even though she did not have a typewriter. That letter states:-

For a variety of reasons, I have decided that it would be best for my money to be looked after professionally. This is not to say I am not ungrateful for what you have done over the years. You have always said I have only to ask for it and I am doing so now. I would like the whole sum to be available by cheque payable to me to be received by midday on Friday 7th January 2000.

I also received a letter from my brother carrying the same date. The lay out to Michael's letter and the typeface were identical to the one allegedly written by Eileen and it also demanded a cheque from me, payable to Eileen, requiring it to be in her hands by 7th January. This letter advised me that Michael had been granted a power of attorney by Eileen to look after all her affairs, with effect from 24th November. This, according to my brother, placed him under a legal obligation to act in the best interests of our stepmother – and only her interests – and if he did not do so he could be sued.

In that letter, Michael went on:-

Eileen has specifically asked me to ensure that her funds, managed by you, are available during your extended absence and for their ultimate return, particularly in the event that any misfortune should befall either of you. I am sure you have managed her funds extremely well in the years since our father's death but it is something I have neither the time nor the expertise to do.

He also noted in that letter:-

Arrangements can be made for safeguards involving either or both of us should you so wish.

Ian and I had been planning a three-month world trip so a meeting was subsequently arranged at our house. Eileen, my brother, Ian and I were present and it was held on 9th January 2000. My brother did most of the talking, keeping total control over the issues. At one stage Eileen spoke, but Michael quickly raised his hand menacingly to stop her, maybe realising that what she was about to say may be to their detriment.

This meeting was recorded by my brother, without my knowledge and consent, as I was to later discover through my own investigations. This is permissible, if it is for personal use, but Michael was then effectively working for the Police, and they are not allowed to record any conversation without the consent of the parties involved, or through an order of a Court. Part of the transcript of that conversation has since been provided to me through my solicitor. It makes interesting reading. I began:-

I want to talk about relationships and what has gone wrong in the past.

The transcript has a break in it at this point. It has never been explained why, but I suspect it was because I was being asked to give Eileen £50,000. I explained:-

With the best will in the world I cannot write a cheque for a large amount today. Investments have been made. I cannot write a cheque for thousands of pounds today.

Michael chipped in:

You are right about drawing a line under the past.

Questioning Michael's motives, I asked Eileen:-

What do I say? Do we turn around and say it wasn't a gift ten years ago? You gave it to me. It was your money and you went on income support.

Eileen then asked:-

Have you got the cheque I made out?

I responded:-

You did not make the cheque out. Dad made the [£50,000] cheque out.

The conversation then turned to the £5000 cheque which Eileen had requested so she could take the trip to Australia. I said:-

We came down October/November time and you said you wanted a cheque for £5000 to go to Australia but I suggested you wait until the end of December. I said I was going to give you a cheque for £5000. What happened in between? Are you still going to Australia?

Eileen said she was and I observed:-

I would suggest £5000 is a lot of money but I can write you a cheque for £5000 today.

The conversation progressed. Eileen said:-

The thing is I really want £10,000. I've got to repay Douggie a lot of money.

I told her I did not have the cash readily available as it was invested but we would discuss the matter again when we came home from our holiday in April.

Eileen continued:-

What if anything happens to you?

I reminded her she had a copy of my will and knew she would be provided for if anything happened.

There is another break in the transcript here. But when it resumed, I am quoted:-

I've talked to you about the money, Eileen. You gave the money to us. It is ours. You are perfectly within your rights to claim income support.

Eileen:-

Yes, but I don't want to live on income support.

I then asked why she applied for this support in the first place. Her response – that I had talked her into it – left me flabbergasted.
There is another break in the transcript, but at this point Michael joined the discussion:-

So really the options are whether you are prepared to give Eileen a lump sum, which is what she would like?

I agreed, but again emphasised it would have to wait till we returned from our holiday:-

We will make a settlement, an agreement about figures. This is why I said to you find out what Eileen needs to live on. Find out what investments she would get for £50,000, £100,000, or £10,000. What does she need? It would be interesting to find out. You're her financial advisor now.

Michael was emphatic. He was not Eileen's financial advisor. 'No, I'm not,' he said insistently.

I continued: -

Find out what she needs to live on so she does not need to stay on income support. I will make a settlement on Eileen when we come back. I'm sorry you don't trust me. I will give you a cheque for £5000 now.

Michael then hit the nail on the head:-

I think that is the hub of the problem, lack of trust.

Eileen agreed to take a cheque for £5000 so she could go to Australia and I agreed we would talk about it more when we returned.

The discussion then returned to the issue of where Eileen would stand if something happened to me, a recurring theme it appeared. I assured her that if the worst was to occur, she would get the money which I had provided for in my will.

Michael butted in eagerly:-

How much? £50,000?

I advised them that there was £70,000 in the codicil. I asked Eileen if she had a copy of the codicil and she said she did not. Again I emphasised the position as I saw it:-

I consider the money mine. I consider it to be a gift.

Michael cut in abruptly again:-

The legal advice is that if the money came after Dad's death...

It was now my turn to interrupt:-

Dad wrote the cheque, long gone, before he died. I remember going down there. I don't know if that was all his money. He could have had £50,000 or £250,000 in Jersey. I don't know. In actual fact was the money in Dad's or Eileen's name?

I, of course, knew the answer to this question but Michael said unconvincingly he did not know, so I asked Eileen the same question. She said she could not remember, although somewhat unconvincingly.

Michael re-entered the fray:-

You told me it was in Eileen's name and you told me Eileen wrote the cheque.

Again it was my turn to reiterate what I had already advised, and what I knew to be true:-

No, Dad wrote the cheque.

Eileen:-

This is what I can't remember because I didn't write the cheque.

That was the position. As the transcript revealed, I had a clear memory of events, but Eileen did not:-

She didn't write the cheque. Dad wrote the cheque, because he had signing authority. As I recall there was no money in Dad's name, not in the flat or anything before he died. He wrote the cheque on Eileen's account from Jersey. I would not have considered or believe he wrote a cheque for every penny there was.

Eileen responded:-

Yes, he did! That was all the money. I have no other money.

I then asked Eileen if she had in fact known my father had given me the £50,000, knowing she was there on the day he made that gift, and she had heard the reasons he provided for doing so.

Watching her begin to form her response, Michael broke in abruptly at this point, raising his hand again to halt her. He clearly didn't want her to reply.

'So is there still an account in Jersey?' he asked.

'I don't know,' I said. Then, trying to get Eileen to respond from a different angle, I said: 'He cleaned the account out then?'

Michael cut in again:-

There wouldn't have been an amount of £50,000 in round figures.

I resumed my questioning: -

So there would have been money left over. What happened to that?

Eileen:-

I have no idea at all. Right I must check up on the Jersey account.

The transcript has another break here but when it resumed, Michael is recorded:-

If it is resolved on your return, there is a codicil in your will which acknowledged £50,000.

By way of clarification, and to ensure there was no misunderstanding, I then said:-

No, it does not acknowledge anything. If you had read my will, if anything happened to Rachel, Ian and I, we left all the rest of our money to the two most dearest people to me who are sat in this room now. You and Eileen. You see what I thought of Eileen. Have you seen the will?

Michael admitted he had seen sections of my will, but not the codicil. I told them clearly I fully acknowledged I did receive money from Dad and Eileen ten years earlier and acknowledged that since then Eileen had been on income support.

I went on to say that if anything happened to me Ian would most likely return to New Zealand and I would not be able to keep my promise to my father. I had therefore ensured money would go to Eileen from my estate.

The taped transcript of our conversation ended there, but I know our conversation continued at our meeting.

I wrote Eileen a cheque for £5000 for her to go to Australia but she never went.

Although I have often wondered why the complete tape was not subsequently sent to my solicitor I am grateful that it had been made, with or without my knowledge, as it clearly sets out my views on the money and it also clearly shows reluctance by Eileen and my brother to repeat the allegation of theft.

Eileen kept diaries which are now all in my brother's hands. The ones covering 1999 and 2005 were withheld although others were subsequently provided to my solicitor, who took notes from them. One such note from the 2000 diary recorded under January stated: 'The day Adrienne and Ian Nairn did me out of my life's savings.' That is extremely odd as this was the month in which I undertook to make a settlement on Eileen, even though the money was gifted to me during 1989. I always wondered why wait eleven years or so to record such a claim – in her 2000 diary?

These diaries make interesting reading. They record the times we met up with Eileen or took her on holiday. There is very little mention of my brother, or of holidays or Christmases our step-mother spent with him.

Eileen made reference in the taped conversation to the fact that she did not know much about the bank account in Jersey, but she only had to refer back to her diaries and the answer would have been clear:-

August 11th 1986 Paid £800 into Jersey
5th March 1987 Pay into Midland Worthing £8856 for Jersey
1st April 1988 Gib money starts today 10.75% 6 months
5th February 1988 Paid into Jersey £1100 – did not give account number. Name of cashier Carol Colvin
21st June 1988 Paid into Jersey £700
1st Feb 1989 Paid into Jersey £202.29
19th July 1989 Wrote to Midland Bank Jersey, putting money into my name only – was joint.

That was 'joint' with my father as it was the week before he died. And finally, something in Eileen's dairy which says it all. On Thursday April 12th 1990 there is an entry:-

J A/c account closed. Adrienne's money.

So it does appear Eileen closed the account herself after deciding not to turn the account into a joint one with me, as she had proposed in a rough draft of a letter dated 30th September 1989. A copy of the scribbled draft letter appears as an appendix in this book.

My brother Michael always maintained the 'J' stood for 'joint', but as I had always known, Eileen always referred to the account as 'Jersey' and that is what the "J" stood for.

Just before our long trip around the world early in 2000 Michael informed me in no uncertain terms we 'would be going nowhere'. He threatened to stop us going on our trip and that he was going to effectively freeze our bank accounts, including Rachel's - and that a Court injunction had been issued against me. Of course there was nothing of the sort. These were only threats as I knew the Court would have advised me if an injunction had been issued.

It also became obvious my brother was saying dreadful things about me to friends and family, and things became difficult with my mother. I didn't mention anything to her for a while, but in the end I felt I had to talk to her about what had developed with Eileen. She did not want to listen, although she was in fact listening to my brother's rants. It seemed obvious to me that my brother intended to get his own way by pushing me out of the family equation through psychological warfare. Brute force was not the only thing he learned to apply masterly in the Army. It was many years before I pieced together exactly what had happened.

Eileen had made a will in 1990, almost a year after my father died, for which I was executor, with a codicil added in June 1999. Both were drawn up by local solicitors and were clearly well thought out. It was to be many years before subsequent wills came into my possession. Our disagreement took place in late August 1999 and, as I was to discover, on 8th November that year Eileen made a new will which is captured on what appears to be pro forma stationery obtainable from any newsagents. This appointed Michael as executor and left all Eileen's real property to him, which in effect left her intestate regarding the remainder of her estate. Later that same month she also granted a general power of attorney to my brother.

On 3rd March 2000, while we were still away, Eileen made yet another will in which she appointed my brother executor, and made him the sole beneficiary of her estate - both real and personal. Her brother-in-law, niece, nephew and three second cousins are only then named in the context that if Michael should predecease Eileen, then her estate was to be divided between them. This will was typed, again on what appeared to be a pro forma document, perhaps obtainable over the internet, and was dated by my brother, clearly showing he was in attendance. No solicitor was involved.

It is interesting that a handwritten note produced later is addressed to 'Mike, my stepson' and is headed 'My third will'. It is dated 2nd January 2000 and listed her intended pecuniary legacies to six relations, with other items to go to her friends Terry and Julia. I say this is interesting because the terms of this written request were not included in Eileen's subsequent version in the series of wills.

I also find it unusual that my stepmother decided to leave her real estate to my brother, because on the same day and typed in the same way - on what also appears to be a pro forma document dated by my brother – she gifted her apartment outright to him. This is known as an 'assignment by way of gift' and clearly indicates my brother was being so rewarded in recognition of him paying off the debts of my father.

As far as I am aware the only debt my father had when he died was to the glaziers for work they did on the patio doors, which I reimbursed my brother for a few months before Eileen gifted the Milford apartment to him.

On my return from our trip, I once again tried to resolve matters, although I may not have been so inclined had I known about Eileen's gift of the apartment to Michael.

Douggie Croshawe dropped a hint about this soon after we returned from our trip, asserting that Eileen had 'dug herself a hole so deep she could not get out of it.'

I was somewhat baffled by his pointed comment, presuming he meant Eileen had fallen under Michael's influence, and she was now too frightened to admit the truth. Douggie, of course, knew about the new will and assignment by way of gift as he was a witness to both. These documents were both dated in Michael's handwriting, proving he was also in attendance.

I concluded that in our absence, Eileen may have made a new will in his favour and that my brother would be the main beneficiary. It was at that moment the realisation came to me there would be no resolution between us, and Michael would undoubtedly wield the powers he had been given under the general power of attorney. My resolve to not capitulate strengthened from that defining moment.

But I was prepared to continue paying Eileen's bills and giving her cash if we could come to an agreement, simply because I had told my father that I would be there for her in her later years.

On 7th August 2000 my cousin Nic tried to resolve things. A meeting was arranged by him to be held at his house but that day was to deliver another shock. My brother handed me a letter, written by my stepmother, which stated 'Adrienne Nairn is a liar, a thief and a cheat.' Michael still has that letter, and it is my belief he has shown it to others from the outset and over many years, despite my denials that there was any truth to Eileen's accusations.

At one point during this 'meeting' Michael lost his temper with Nic – a frightening experience. Nic told Michael that perhaps our father had given me the cheque in 1989 because I had not had the benefit of a private school education, but he had. My brother absolutely blew his top at that suggestion, and it is one of the few times I have seen him lose his cool. It was true that Michael did not have such educational benefits, but that was his own fault as he had been given every opportunity to 'go private'.

Michael regained his composure pretty quickly, but I was certainly glad I made Nic promise not to leave me alone in the room with my brother as I feared him deeply by then. I was also grateful Nic's wife and Ian were within calling distance.

That meeting ended with me indicating I would send Eileen a really nice bouquet of flowers as a 'sorry' for the disagreement that had evolved. As usual I was willing to make the first move. But once again I reiterated that I was gifted the money and felt I had nothing to apologise for.

My brother then drove down to Milford to visit Eileen and when I got home there was a message on the answer phone informing me that Eileen did not want flowers and nor did she ever want to speak to me again. The message was left by Michael, not Eileen.

This is a situation which has not been helped by Michael. I have always believed that if, at any stage in any of these proceedings, he had told Eileen to get over the fact the £50,000 had been actually gifted to me, she would have done so without doubt.

In 2001 Eileen made yet another new will, again appointing Michael as executor and the main beneficiary, but this time she left bequests to her niece and brother-in-law. She expressly excluded me. This will was drawn up by my brother's solicitors in Northampton, many miles from Milford where my stepmother lived.

About this time Eileen wrote to Rachel, but that letter – which was in her hand this time and not typed – was only produced years later. This letter is very significant in the context of what Eileen had previously been claiming. She stated:-

Before your grandfather died in 1989 he gave Adrienne the sum of £50,000 of my money without my knowledge for the purpose of looking after me financially.

Of course this appeared to be in distinct contrast with what she had been telling Michael. She also admitted in this letter that I had looked after her financially. But then she also went on to note she felt she had shown me gratitude by paying for our holidays abroad. The reality was something else, as I had paid for all the holidays she took with us and Douggie had paid for his own trips. Indeed, if she had paid for our holidays as she claimed one would have to ask why Eileen was on income support?

Rachel, of course, knew the truth from the beginning so Eileen's complaints would have fallen on deaf ears – if she had received the letter, but she didn't. That letter actually ended up in my brother's hands, although there has never been an explanation of how that happened. I doubt it was a copy as Eileen would surely not have hand-written a letter and then copied it out again in long hand when it was intended only for Rachel's eyes.

I was also later to discover Eileen had signed a typed statement asserting that she 'had no knowledge of any gift, deed or assignment from my father' and that it was only after his death I told her about the money. She went on to say I had managed all her financial affairs from his death. This defies belief as the entries in her own diaries record details of the Jersey bank account, what money was paid in and when and the date and reason for its closure. The dairies are clearly in Eileen's own hand.

~ *Eighteen* ~

I tried to keep something going with Eileen by writing letters, starting off nicely while still trying to resolve things sensibly. I tried to explain that one doesn't usually say people have stolen money ten years after the alleged event and I also indicated that, if she considered the £50,000 actually belonged to her, she would not be entitled to receive income support.

I telephoned her cousin Ted Farmer, and her niece Dawn Boden, to try and get them to talk to her, to no avail. If either of them spoke with Eileen about this matter, I never heard the outcome.

So, in an effort to resolve things from my point of view, I reported Eileen's circumstances to Social Services, hoping an investigation would be initiated. I felt, if nothing else, the wicked accusation of theft against me would be resolved.

I had previously warned Eileen I would report her to Social Services. Michael had by then been working for Northants Police for some years as a firearms officer and I suspected they would not investigate one of their own.

I had always felt strongly Eileen should not have been receiving income support if she seriously considered the £50,000 belonged to her. Having been so ridiculously accused of stealing her money, I felt it was time to initiate professional enquiries of some sort before things really got out of hand. By then I had really come to fear Michael, knowing what I did about his past.

My confidential reporting of Eileen, via the social security hotline, took place in August 2001 yet it seems she was not visited until the end of October. She denied being in possession of investment funds, but she was very quickly able to deduce, quite rightly, that I had been the informant.

As a matter of interest, the Social Services investigator recorded, in a document produced some years later, that Eileen's penthouse apartment was 'very palatial' and he found it particularly 'hard to believe she could keep it up to its current standard on income support and her pension alone'. At that meeting the investigator stated Eileen had denied being in possession of any additional funds and that her late husband, Maurice Lobb, had given Mrs Nairn £50,000 to look after her but Mrs Nairn had kept it for herself. He also noted he was going to speak with Eileen's stepson, and he recorded 'someone in the family is lying, but I know not who.'

Some of the documents relating to this investigation were provided to me later and there was another note I found particularly interesting. This records that having found Eileen's apartment 'very palatial' on his first visit, only two weeks later the investigating officer inexplicably stated:

On looking at the flat a second time I could see that it was living on past glories and I am not so sure now she does have additional capital.

He also asked her outright about any other banks accounts she had in existence and she then stated she only had one and that she had been selling off possessions to raise extra money.

That investigator should, of course, have asked if she had any previous bank accounts, to which the answer should have been that she indeed had had one in Jersey. Knowing what we know now, I also have to wonder why Eileen did not ask my brother for financial help rather than having to sell off her possessions. He had after all been gifted the £600,000 penthouse apartment by that stage.

It is also interesting to note that years later, when the Social Services New Forest District Council files were divulged to me, one document - dated 15th November 2001- was withheld. That was the same date as the investigator changed his mind regarding the palatial surroundings of Eileen's apartment. I have never been able to obtain this document.

Through persistence, I was provided with letters from the New Forest District Council to my brother clearly indicating I was the 'confidential' informant. But they still refuse to disclose the one document clearly referring to me personally. I put my complaint to the tribunal but they refused to divulge the information based on the following:-

Having examined the withheld material, it was found that some of the information was personal information relating to the appellant which could not be disclosed under FOIA since section 40(1) provides that information is exempt from disclosure under the Act if it constitutes personal data of which the applicant is the data subject. The Respondent further observed that it was open to the appellant to exercise her rights under the Data Protection Act to access such data. He further found that the rest of the withheld material was exempt under section 41 (1) since it was obtained by a public authority in circumstances where disclosure would constitute an actionable breach of confidence and the balance of public interest was in preserving that confidence.

I did receive what I regarded as insulting apology from the New Forest District Council for disclosing my name to Eileen and my brother. This council seems to think that apology absolves it, but the tribunal told me I could have taken civil action.

All this left me questioning the vehemently defended concept of public bodies protecting the identities of their informants.

This incident also left me wondering if this council was really interested in uncovering benefit fraudsters. Those who fund this local authority could be justified in asking the same question. The New Forest District Council went on to close its file, indicating that, in its opinion, Eileen was not in possession of this particular money, which my brother had corroborated. The council also indicated it would not get involved in what it viewed as a family feud, and it felt there was a lack of evidence to show Eileen had committed benefit fraud.

My dreams intensified.

There was no resolution to the on-going disagreement with Eileen, so Ian and I decided to move back to New Zealand. Rachel had been living in Australia for six years by then and we had considered setting up home there too. We decided, however, to go to New Zealand for a three month trial run so to speak and stay in one place initially. We opted for Taupo, in the Central North Island which is a beautiful town on the edge of New Zealand's largest lake.

We had earlier been looking at house swaps and by coincidence, while on the computer, I found someone who was offering their house in Taupo in exchange for one in the United Kingdom. In reality the house swap was never going to work because we both wanted summers in each country. But I did phone the potential house-swapper, Anna, and we met her and her husband for dinner. Anna was to become my soul mate, surrogate sister and confidante, a relationship we have to this day.

We liked Taupo from the moment we arrived and having Rachel in Australia certainly made our decision to move to the southern hemisphere a lot easier.

If we thought we would be leaving behind Eileen, my brother and the disagreement which had been festering, then we were clearly mistaken. The campaign continued unabated and in fact intensified, with Michael telling my cousin Nic that if ever I set foot in the United Kingdom again I would be arrested by three different Police forces! I should not have been concerned by this as I knew I had not done anything wrong, but I did fear some trumped up charge could be waiting for me. I was also intrigued by Michael's assertion to Nic so I wrote to Northants Police, my brother's employer, asking if I was a wanted woman.

Correspondence, which can only be regarded as bizarre, then followed. First of all there was a demand for £10 for a basic computer search of what the Police may have held on me in their database in the context of outstanding arrest warrants. I flatly refused to pay but persevered and reiterated I understood I was a wanted person and was effectively handing myself in. The eventual reply indicated, quite clearly, there was no record whatsoever of me on the top ten wanted list in the United Kingdom or any other such list no matter the ranking. I wondered why the Police had not pulled my brother in to ask him why he had falsely accused me of theft, and why he had said I was wanted. What Michael had told Nic was a cruel move to scare me off and perhaps, one aimed at encouraging me to give Eileen the money. It did not escape my attention that had I done so, Michael himself would have ended up with most of it, being the main beneficiary of our stepmother's will. This would have been the ultimate irony, given that he knew he would also receive the entire benefit of the £600,000 penthouse apartment.

While this on-going disagreement with Eileen and Michael should not have affected my relationship with my mother it did. We always had a good relationship, although my brother loves to relate we did have a blip in our relationship in the late1980s. That was something I think both Mother and I regretted because once I picked up the phone and apologised we got back on track.

My brother has related recently that he was the one who patched things up between Mother and I after five years. That is untruthful as it was my cousin Nic who brokered that 'peace deal'.

My step-father Bill had multiple sclerosis and Mother cared for him throughout. It was hard work, but while we were living in Warminster they came to visit. Ian drove up to Bridlington to get them and after their visit took them home again. We went to stay with them too a lot and had many good times.

Eventually Mother didn't want to go away with my step-father. It was very hard work and he was not nice to her a lot of the time. We tried to tell him he had to be more caring toward her, because if anything happened to her, he would be lost but that mostly fell on deaf ears.

It also became too much hard work for my mother to come to Warminster with my step-father, but she needed holidays and after Bill had spent some time in a nursing home after her heart attack he refused to go in one again. So Ian and I went up twice to look after Bill in their home while she was away for a break with her sister, my Aunty Ruth. The first time we went Bill had 'an accident'. When my mother phoned that evening to see if everything was alright I told her she had forgotten to tell us her husband was incontinent! She replied 'I knew you would find out soon enough!'

On one occasion when we went to stay my mother gave us a few items – glasses, dishes and the like. Thinking she was not in the room I told Ian that perhaps we should get it in writing that she had given us these items. Unfortunately Mother heard me and snapped back quickly that I should not be so stupid. Hopefully she was not about to gift me something and then turn around and say she wanted it back ten years later.

Just before we moved to New Zealand, Rachel returned to the United Kingdom for Christmas 2001 with her then boyfriend. She wanted to sort out her belongings in our house and to say goodbye to her Granny and Grandpa as it was unlikely she would be travelling that far quite so often. The four of us went to Bridlington to visit Mother and Bill. Ian and I stayed at the house, but there was not enough room for Rachel and her boyfriend. Uncle Trevor had died by then and we thought Aunty Ruth could have had them to stay in her large house but she did not offer so Rachel and her boyfriend stayed in a bed and breakfast guest house nearby. We had a lot of laughs on that trip also and I took photos of Mother with tears running down her face. On the last evening, she cried real tears, and many of them, realising we were all probably leaving the United Kingdom for good. As much as I would have liked to, I was still not able to talk to her about the problems I was having with Michael.

Mother eventually had to put Bill into a nursing home and he died not long after. I got a very curt, descriptive account of the funeral from Michael, one that ended like this:-

A reply is neither expected nor required.

~ *Nineteen* ~

Before leaving the United Kingdom, we packed up everything – filled containers with our possessions – and put the house in Warminster on the open market. We had decided not to take our car to New Zealand, so bought one immediately we arrived as we were to tour the South Island while waiting for our belongings to arrive by sea.

We had decided to rent a house to give ourselves time to get to know Taupo and the surrounding area and to see which part of the town we wanted to live in. In this task Anna proved to be absolutely marvellous. For Ian the novelty of looking at houses very rapidly wore off and we knew we would not be in a position to buy anything until our Warminster house sold. Anna and I looked at houses together and she would tell me the good areas from her perspective, drawing a map then marking the less desirable ones in pink. She often quipped that if we bought in a 'bad' area, she would not come and visit!

We actually liked the place we were renting. It was nicely laid out with a picturesque view of the lake and mountains and we considered buying it but having to share a garden with the rental flat below us was not ideal. Selling our English house was proving to be somewhat problematic. Although prospective purchasers were certainly in abundance they either just did not have the money, or were in a similar position to us, having to sell their own property first. So for our first nine months in Taupo we continued to rent.

House prices were rising in New Zealand at the time and as it turned out, the timing of our decision to settle in Ian's home country was exactly the right one since we got three dollars and 40 cents for each of our British pounds at that time. With the strength of New Zealand's currency, it is now only two dollars to the pound, or thereabouts.

Whilst the weakness of the dollar was working in our favour we could see house prices were rising dramatically in New Zealand and I suggested to Ian we should buy a house, any house, just to get on the 'ladder'. We found something we felt would suit our needs.

At that time we had an offer on our Warminster house, but knowing the disappointments we had in the past we were not banking on that. So we agreed to the purchase in Taupo, and only ten days later, our English house sold, much to our relief. Good old Douggie would have said it was 'Sod's law'. Everything really does happen for a reason, and we love the house we have in Taupo and have no interest in moving. Our house is compact, the property is easy to manage and we can walk to the town centre. Best of all it has the most wonderful view of the lake and the three mountains which rise majestically to the south. I think of this often as Ian said seriously we would never get a view of both with our limited financial resources! For once, he was proved wrong.

When I first arrived in Taupo I visited a clairvoyant. I'm not serious about that sort of thing, but Rachel and I had done so previously for a bit of fun, tossing all sorts of silly questions into the hat, such as when she would get married, whether she would have a long life or how many babies she would have? My questions varied from time to time.

This particular clairvoyant seemed to be highly regarded so I went along. No-one knew me at that time as I was new to town and no-one had any background information. There was no point in going to see someone like that if they had any prior knowledge. At first the clairvoyant chatted and I was clever enough to leave it to her to tell me things. Then she opened the floor for questions from me, whereupon I asked about my mother, step-father, step-mother and brother. She told me that my step-father would 'go when he wanted to go'. Interestingly, Bill died only a few weeks later, after having been put into a nursing home which he hated. The clairvoyant then told me that my mother was elderly, was set in her ways and was vulnerable. She then told me my step-mother had 'been born with a silver knife in her mouth'. That expression described Eileen particularly well, in my view.

Without prompting from me, the clairvoyant spoke about my brother, with an expression on her face which surprised me. With venom she declared: 'Your brother is a shit.' That is not one word of a lie – that is exactly what she said. I left that session thinking 'how did she know?'

On arrival in Taupo I had decided I did not want paid employment so I did voluntary work instead. Before I could do so I required training and this is where I met lovely Brenda. As it turned out she had just been widowed and we became good friends.

On the day we moved from our rental house to our new home Brenda turned up with a big tray loaded with sandwiches, flasks of coffee and cakes. There was more than enough for us – and the removal men. Brenda was destined to feature very strongly in our future lives.

Having enjoyed his trip to New Zealand with Ian in 1999 our widowed friend Mike decided to return and did so in 2003, staying with us this time. One night I asked Brenda to dinner. The rest, as they say, is history. Their relationship flourished and in 2005 they married on the beach in Taupo. I have never seen a couple so happy. They loved each other so much but unfortunately it was not to last. In July 2011 Brenda died of a brain tumour. As Mike was to put it 'the fairy tale ended'.

Mike is really the brother I wish I had and whether he stays in New Zealand or not I will always be there for him. I know the feeling is reciprocated.

Ian suffered some worrying medical symptoms in 2002, but unfortunately they were mis-diagnosed. These symptoms persisted and eventually he was scheduled for a colonoscopy. Not knowing the medical system in New Zealand and, upon being told it was probably nothing to worry about, we waited, and then waited some more. Overall we waited for nine months for a date for tests and by the time he got them the worst was confirmed – Ian had colon cancer.

At that time we were due to go to Australia to visit Rachel but we were told an operation could not wait even a couple of weeks and on 1st April 2004 Ian underwent an operation in Rotorua Hospital, a much bigger city about one hour from where we lived. The operation itself was deemed a success, but Ian was very ill as he contracted pneumonia in the hospital.

Ian was in Rotorua Hospital for two weeks but when we arrived home, sheer delight was to be had as Rachel arrived unexpectedly. She really wanted to visit her Dad and support him. Of course, Ian should not have had to wait for so long for the colonoscopy. We know that in hindsight, and Ian received profuse apologies from his doctor, the surgeon, and even the hospital. Receiving an apology would never have happened in England!

Although this was a difficult time for us, we coped, thanks to the wonderful friends we had and the support they provided.

While Ian was in hospital I travelled to Rotorua most days, only to find a dinner waiting for me on the doorstep on return. Following his operation, Ian had a nine month course of chemotherapy, once a week every week. Fortunately he was able to have this in Taupo rather than having to travel to Rotorua.

~ *Twenty* ~

Just as we thought our lives had settled again, the Eileen and Michael saga emerged again and this time the action came from a totally unexpected quarter – the Taupo Police!

On this particular day there was a knock at the door. I was out but Ian was in.

The Taupo Police officer told Ian there had been a complaint lodged against me, and it had been passed from Hampshire Police, to Interpol, and on to the New Zealand Police! He told Ian I was being accused of harassing my step-mother and that it was 'best I stopped'. The officer didn't actually want to see me, but advised Ian he had inherited the complaint and it had been sitting on his desk for three months. He merely wanted to clear his desk. He was not interested, but I was.

Arriving home I turned around and hot-footed it to the Police station to discuss the matter. It was there I learned Interpol was involved. I just couldn't believe it. Whatever would have warranted the intervention of an international crime detection agency?

From what I was told it appeared the thrust of the so-called harassment complaint was that I had reported my step-mother to Social Services. I had, allegedly, written nasty letters to her, and for good measure was being accused of sending anonymous letters to some of her neighbours, posted from New Zealand. I made the point – most strongly – that if I wanted to harass anyone in the United Kingdom I would have had the incriminating letters posted there, not from the other side of the world. I had a very pleasant friendly chat with that officer and he did not appear to take offence when I suggested that surely he, the Hampshire Police, and Interpol had better things to do. This was a family feud which had been simmering for years and it was not, I would have thought, a matter for Police forces in two different countries. The police officer agreed, but said he had to be seen doing the right thing.

As this action had not in any way been initiated by me, I took the opportunity to tell him the whole story, including that I had only replied to letters received from Eileen demanding money from me. He did not show me any paperwork relating to the complaint, although when he was flicking through his file, I saw a copy of a will and copies of letters and emails from New Forest District Council. I remember it was quite a thick file.

When I produced my own account of the matter, the officer seemed to be really quite astounded. I then added I took my brother's threats towards me as being serious and with ill-intent.

Ian's situation was very worrying for us at that time because of his ill health. My mother knew how ill Ian was and I assumed she had told Michael. The week the Police officer called, Ian was so stressed he could not have his chemotherapy. The nurses just could not find a vein as he was so uptight.

At that time, my dreams about my brother had already turned into nightmarish events – murderous in effect.

As the Police had been involved – but not at my instigation – I suggested one of their liaison officers should visit Eileen in England. I considered this to be a step in the right direction in the context that the truth of the matter may at last come to light. I was given the name of Detective Constable Bob Ashton, the International Liaison Officer, and took the trouble of writing to him, pointing out the facts and adding that I welcomed any intervention or investigation. I also indicated I was surprised Interpol was involved in what seemed to be a family dispute. I also indicated I suspected my brother was abusing his position as a Police employee. In that letter I said I was making a formal complaint against my step-mother and brother for their harassment, including continual requests for money and for making defamatory statements. Defence had turned on attack and I was glad to have been handed the golden opportunity of disclosing – and then testing – the evidence I had collated over the preceding years.

I had by then uncovered evidence that my brother had shown several people the letter my step-mother wrote branding me ' a liar and a cheat' and I suggested to DC Bob Ashton that someone go and have a private word with my step-mother, without my brother being present, to try and get to the bottom of the false allegations. I also suggested they talk to Douggie, who knew the truth of the matter.

It is interesting to note that while all this was going on, my brother was arrogant enough to write me a letter in which he invited Ian, Rachel and I to join him in Harrogate to celebrate Mother's eightieth birthday. I did not think this would be a very good idea and we did not return to England for that event.

In the meantime, Bob Ashton wrote back to me, advising the Police did have family liaison officers and crime reduction officers but that their role was not compatible with this situation. He declined to make any comment on the 'rift' as he called it, but added the Police tried to remain impartial in family disputes. It is a pity Hampshire Police didn't abide by this same philosophy initially. He advised me to make my formal harassment complaint to the Police in New Zealand. I am not one to waste Police time and as this line of enquiry would again necessitate the intervention of Interpol, I advised him that any alleged crime could be reported to any Police station. As such, I was formally reporting the crimes that had been committed against me to Hampshire Constabulary. Subsequently Bob Ashton informed me that no report of any crime - stolen monies or otherwise - had ever been reported by my step-mother or my brother.

I persisted with the Hampshire Police, reminding them I was not the one who had involved them in the first place. In my view, their involvement would have emanated from my brother. Needless to say I then received a reply indicating I must make a formal complaint to the Professional Standards Department of Hampshire Police.

My complaint eventually ended up in the hands of Inspector John Heath. I wrote him a long letter conveying the basis of my complaint and unhappiness at the way Hampshire Police had dealt with the matter. Inspector Heath's reply related the manner in which Police enquiries had been made concerning the harassment complaint against me, but there was no official accusation of theft or otherwise lodged against me and he advised he had no knowledge of any letter branding me a liar and a thief . What he was able to confirm was that my brother was present throughout the original interview with my step-mother. In fact my brother made the statement to the reporting officer because my step-mother was too embarrassed to discuss it.

Inspector Heath advised me that Police are under a duty to act when incidents are reported, but they decided they 'did not wish to be drawn into a family dispute and more importantly did not wish to be used as part of such a dispute.' This left me again wondering why they had agreed to become involved in the first place. After all Interpol was brought into the picture by Hampshire Police. My response was that violent crimes often flow out of family disputes.

The response from Inspector Heath did not answer all my questions so I persisted requesting, among other things, that Eileen be interviewed and asked whether £50,000 had been stolen from her at all, and if so, whether I had done so. I also insisted that reporting anyone to Social Services did not constitute harassment. If one honestly believed a crime has been committed, as I did, then one was at liberty to report it. Indeed the local councils urged them to do so, especially when it may involve benefit fraud.

I also asked the Police to check whether any injunctions had been taken out against me as alleged by my brother and whether he made an appointment to see the manager of my former employers, NatWest Bank, in the name of the Police.

In relation to the latter issue I actually wrote to Michael's former employer, Northants Police. That was the Constabulary he named when making an appointment to see my former bank manager. Northants simply forwarded my letter on to Thames Valley Police as my brother had by then moved to that Constabulary. That force sent a short reply, stating Michael no longer worked for them and there was no evidence of misuse of position. Thames Valley Police then put it quite plainly that they would not reply to any further correspondence from me regarding the issue.

Inspector Heath then stopped writing to me, so I sent my official complaint to the Independent Police Complaints Commission. It went back to Hampshire Police Professional Standards Department. The roundabout had been completed but that did not stop me sending emails in a bid to get my issues addressed. It was, I believed, an extraordinarily farcical situation as I was simply trying to find out who I could complain to in the circumstances. No-one was prepared to freely answer that question, preferring to play pass the proverbial buck with my then-taut emotions.

After what had seemed like an interminable period of time, I finally received communications from Chief Superintendent Derek Stevens. He duly appointed Inspector Geoff King and the investigation he conducted brought out some seriously interesting facts.

Firstly, in the background information, Inspector King's report indicated that Mrs Eileen Lobb's late husband, Maurice Lobb, had transferred £50,000 to the complainant – namely me – in trust at some point prior to his demise. The report goes on to state that:-

This had only become apparent to Michael Lobb when the family dispute occurred. Mr Lobb thereafter became involved in attempts to recover that part of his late father's estate on behalf of his stepmother.

This is extremely interesting because the money was not transferred under trust and the Police report is in error on that matter. The Police report then went on to suggest that Eileen had been suffering financial hardship.

Another most intriguing fact surfaced through the depths of murky deceit. I had, as earlier recounted, been accused of writing letters to Eileen's neighbours, the residents of Richmond Court. According to this Police report, these letters were all said to have been 'written in the same hand' and that they had all been posted from the same huge postal region where I live in New Zealand. But when I was eventually granted access to these letters, years later, I found they were all typed, not hand-written at all. I don't know why I was astonished as little should have surprised me by then, but I was. So much for honest and transparent Police investigations and factual reports!

Sometime later I did indeed write a letter to the residents in a bid to refute the story of the harassment I was being accused of by Eileen. These letters were signed by me, as was the case with any correspondence I produced and I arranged for a friend to post them in the UK. One neighbour replied, directly to me, advising the neighbours had received anonymous letters but they had then been told that these had been sent by a 'niece living in New Zealand'. This left me wondering if this was an attempt to discredit both Dawn and myself at the same time – I lived in New Zealand, but she was the niece.

~ *Twenty One* ~

The conclusion of the Professional Standards Department investigation was not a surprise to me, but the unfolding deceit was beginning to take a toll on me. My naïvety of trusting the Police then started to diminish, as nightmares of my brother torturing me by psychological warfare then began to depict him murdering me. Sleep was difficult as I tossed the unbelievable facts around my head.

I have learned that the officer investigating who lodged the original alleged harassment complaint against me was unsure how to proceed, given I lived in New Zealand. He subsequently sought advice and was told to pass the report on to Interpol. My complaint against the Police concerned was not upheld, but there still has been no conclusion as to why a report of alleged fraud is deemed to be harassment.

Inspector Heath was merely given a rap on the knuckles for failing to respond to one of my emails, although this was merely viewed as being 'discourteous'. I imagined at the time the rap was more of a slap and tickle!

Undaunted, I persisted, raising the following points:-

i. Although the family dispute concerned the sum of £50,000, it did not constitute part of my late father's estate. That money came from Eileen Lobb's account in Jersey and there was no suggestion originally that it was to be held by me under trust.

ii. Eileen had never been in financial hardship. She had been receiving income support since 1990 and made no complaint to anyone about financial worries.

iii. The only allegation of harassment resulted from my correspondence to the New Forest District Council and that should have been kept confidential. The informant clearly believed a crime had been committed.

iv. If someone hands over monies to be held under trust – the words used in the Police report - and does not declare the money to the income support office and then receives financial assistance that may be considered to be Social Security fraud.

v. Statements 1 and 2 were referred to in the Police report, but whatever they were, they were they were never supplied to me and I therefore requested copies of them. It would appear statement 1 could have been made by Michael Lobb referring to the sum of £50,000 being transferred by my father, the late Maurice Lobb, in trust prior to his demise and statement 2 could have been made by Eileen Lobb disclosing the matter to Michael Lobb.

> It would appear that the sum of £50,000 was transferred by the late Mr Maurice Lobb to the complainant in trust at some point prior to his demise [see statement 1]. However this only became apparent to the complainant's brother, Michael Lobb, in 1999 when his step-mother and sister had a family dispute and it was disclosed to him by Mrs Lobb [see statement 2].

vi. Copies of unsigned letters received by Eileen's neighbours should be provided to me because they were allegedly written in my hand. I also asked to see Exhibit 7, which would appear to be a statement made by my brother alleging that my treatment of his elderly step-mother was causing her considerable anxiety and distress. Again this exhibit was never produced to me.

vii. Buck-passing seemed to be occurring by the bucket load.

viii. Why did the Police say they do not get involved in family disputes when violent crimes in many circumstances are usually caused by family disputes? This was clearly one such family dispute.

ix. Why did Inspector Heath not answer all my questions?

x. Why was my step-mother Eileen Lobb interviewed with my brother, Michael Lobb present?

I sent my queries to Derek Stevens, regarding what I considered to be bad policing. Unsurprisingly, he did not reply.

My decision was to try my luck with the Independent Police Commission. Although I felt this was also probably a waste of time, I had to try. The reply failed to surprise me either. The IPCC found there was no evidence of the Police failing to consider all of the relevant evidence, or that the conclusions formed by them were in any way unreasonable. The decision was final, but the questions I had put still had not been answered.

I then wrote a formal letter to the Hampshire Constabulary making a complaint on behalf of Mrs Eileen Lobb. In it, I indicated that monies had been stolen from her, with the inference being they had been stolen by me. I did this in an attempt to bring the matter into the open and to give the Police an opportunity to do their job.

Eileen provided a statement as part of the investigation which obviously ensued:-

I do not wish to make a complaint of theft to the Police. The only sum of £50,000 that I have had involvement with was in 1989 when that amount was transferred to Adrienne Nairn by my late husband. The purpose of that money was to provide for me in later years. To the best of my knowledge Mrs Nairn still has this money. I cannot understand why Mrs Nairn has written to the Police about this. I can only state that the contents of the letter are incorrect.

The statement was signed by Eileen and witnessed by Douggie Croshawe. But it raised a number of significant questions. The first is why my step-mother gifted her apartment to my brother in consideration of my late father's debts, especially as I had reimbursed Michael for the glaziers? The second is why Eileen had made accusations in writing that I was a thief? And lastly, if she had a large amount of money tucked away to provide for herself in her later years, why had she claimed income support?

I forwarded a copy of the Police letter to the New Forest District Council and asked the officials if they knew about the transfer of funds. I also asked them why they disclosed information I had given in confidence?

The response was from one Charlotte Lee who advised me that Mr Macfarlane, the original investigator, had retired and the Council was therefore not going to comment any further on the matter.

I do rather lose track of all the complaints and appeals I have made against the Police and other authorities involved to date, but needless to say, none have been upheld. I did my best to frame my complaints correctly, but by then I was beginning to feel for the first time that my resilience was waning. Rightly or wrongly, to me it looked like my brother was getting his calculated, battle-hardened way, having involved his Police colleagues to cover his tracks. I felt I couldn't win against any of the authorities. The utter bureaucracy, lack of professionalism and the time-wasting correspondence had drained me completely. The nightmarish scenes of murderous intent didn't help but I was determined not to allow my brother to live rent free in my head – hero or not.

~ *Twenty Two* ~

While things on the home front had settled and Ian had recovered from his surgery the relationship with Mother deteriorated rapidly. Mother had a fall in her garden and as the story goes she laid there for six hours before my cousin Madeleine found her.

I have been told Madeleine had a hard job persuading my brother to telephone me to let me know what had happened, but eventually he did. I then got updates on Mother's condition, but it is fair to say they were concise and professional, not ones supplied with brotherly love.

I sent emails about Mother and in one asked why she didn't have a personal alarm, to activate in cases of emergencies. She later acquired one, but it should not surprise anyone to learn I was criticised by my brother for not suggesting it earlier.

Finally, I got an email from Michael stating:-

You are under the misapprehension you are being consulted. You are not, you are merely being advised.

When my mother returned home from hospital the phone conversations between us got increasingly difficult. Sometimes she would be fine but on other occasions she would start on about 'Eileen's money'. It was obvious by then she believed Michael's side of the story, not mine.

In 2007 Rachel married Jamie, a great guy. We invited Mother and Aunty Ruth to the wedding in Sydney. They did not attend but I couldn't believe Mother's wedding gift – a dented, dirty, silver milk jug, obviously just plucked from her cabinet. The contrast in her attitude was unbelievable – when Rachel bought her first apartment five years earlier my mother had given her £3000!

Times have changed a lot in the way people get married these days. Many have been living together for a while – as Rachel and Jamie had before they tied the knot. They do things their way, often paying for the wedding themselves and certainly arranging the big ceremony in the way they want it.

But I liked to follow some elements of tradition so I insisted that, as Rachel's parents, we would pay. That said, I suppose we did it the modern way by saying we would give them a lump sum to spend and if there was a surplus they could use it as they wished. If it was going to cost more, that would be up to them. I wanted Rachel to have the wedding I never had, and in that respect I wanted the invitations to come from Ian and I, and they did.

Ian and Adrienne Nairn request the company of ...

The formal responses however were to go directly to Rachel in Sydney, which seemed more sensible as we resided in New Zealand. However Mother responded directly to us and in doing so she was making it obvious she was not about to follow simple and reasonable instructions:-

I shall respond to invitations in the way I was brought up – to the bride's parents.

I think my Aunty Ruth must have had a different nanny to my mother because she didn't respond until well after the requested date and she declined. She did wish the happy couple well via Ian and I, but there was no gift or even a card for Rachel and Jamie.

Their wedding was beautiful, being held in the Rose Gardens in Sydney, followed by a small reception on the harbour front. It was perfect.

~ *Twenty Three* ~

In early 2008, I was actually having a nice chat with Mother by phone when she told me she had been in hospital following a heart attack. I was annoyed I had not been told and phoned my aunt to ask why not. She said I was being rude to her but when I said I was only being firm, things turned from bad to worse. Aunty Ruth said Mother had only had an angina attack, but even so it would have been nice to have been told the correct diagnosis.

Always being the one who tried hard to make amends I attempted to apologise to my aunt for my comments, but she put the phone down on me. I then phoned Mother but as Michael was visiting we only had a stilted conversation about 'building bridges'.

At this point, I should say that Mother had told me previously that my brother had taped conversations of meetings we had with Eileen. Why my brother would make my mother listen to them I did not know, but it did not concern me as I had nothing to hide.

But that gave me an idea, that I should tape any conversations myself in future. This is perfectly legal if the recordings are for personal use. I have a tape of the conversation which involved 'building bridges' and I have a recording of my aunt putting the phone down after she insisted I talk with Michael and after she accused me of acting despicably toward my mother. I also have tapes of my mother saying the strangest things.

I often wondered why my aunt took the attitude she did and whether she was afraid of Michael and what he might do. He did help her out of a very difficult situation once. This came after the horrifying Dunblane massacre, the result of which was that gun laws were being changed. The Police issued an amnesty allowing the public to hand in unlicensed firearms but after the deadline Ruth approached Michael and admitted she had a small pistol hidden away. Uncle Trevor had given her this pistol many years before for her own protection but it was unlicensed and she had not handed it in. I am not sure if Michael did give it to the Police, or just threw it in a river, but Ruth was off the hook.

Not long after, I again phoned my mother but Michael answered and told me that Aunty Ruth was upset about my call. He claimed Mother and Ruth were very frail. I again talked about building bridges as being the best way forward.

Michael responded by saying our mother was his primary objective and whatever our differences, we could overlook them in relation to her affairs.

I agreed, saying Mother's health was also my concern but I reinforced I had been upset I had not been told about her illness.

Michael: It was Mother's express wish.
Adrienne: But in the end, she did tell me about it. She did want me to know. For Mother's sake we need to have a relationship.
Michael: Fine.
Adrienne: OK?
Michael: Yes.
Adrienne: I'll talk to Mother.
Michael: She does not want to talk to you.
Adrienne: Why?
Michael: You'll have to ask her yourself. I am following Mother's wishes.

Michael continued to talk - about her heart murmur, holidays, and the Masonic Home in Exeter she would eventually move into. The questions and answers continued:-

Me: Have you looked at other homes?
Michael: No, they are all the same.

More general chit chat followed, with me trying to be friendly. But he then concluded, saying he was not going to interfere with anyone else's relationships.

During another conversation my mother asked me how I was getting on with building bridges with Ruth. I said I would phone her but my mother did not want me to do that, suggesting I had not bothered with my aunt for years.

'Don't start with Ruth, start with Michael,' she urged. 'When are you going to ring him?' I told her it was Michael's turn to phone me and what did she want me to do? She said she was sick of it all and did not care any more.

What I did not know then, and of course no-one had told me, was that my mother and brother knew something I did not. I was not to get to the answer until I arrived in England a short time later, having decided to go and sort out the issues face-to-face.

~ *Twenty Four* ~

I did not advise anyone I had returned, nor the reason for my visit, surprise being one of the age-old forms of winning a war. But the surprise, or more correctly the shock, was to come for me, not Mother and Michael.

One of the first calls I made on arrival in England was to Eileen's apartment, but rather than finding my step-mother in that freshly-redecorated penthouse, I found tenants in residence. Imagine my horror when they told me Eileen had died late the previous year, and her step-son now owned the apartment, having 'bought it off her some years previously.'

I decided at this stage not to visit Douggie, as I thought he would just telephone my brother and let him know I was in the country. Whether such a meeting would have made a difference I shall never know because six days later he died.

I started making enquiries and soon found the title of the penthouse apartment had been officially transferred to my brother - for nil consideration - only a few months before Eileen's death.

I then visited my mother but on turning up on the doorstep I was informed I was not welcome and she would not let me stay. She made her displeasure very apparent. I recorded the conversation because of her hostility. Even today listening to that conversation is distressing for me and I won't disclose the full contents unless necessary, but this is a record of part of it:-

I'm not pleased with you, the way you've behaved. What you have done? Don't you know Eileen has died? I wish you hadn't come. You have no idea how to build bridges. You can't give Eileen her money back now. I knew you had Eileen's money. You are a manipulator. You made a load of money out of it. You put it in a joint account with Eileen. It's your money – go to a B&B, and don't go calling on Ruth. You've had a wasted journey.

When I suggested someone could have at least let Rachel know her

Granny had died Mother retorted that Eileen was not her Granny, she was and she certainly was not dead!

Mother then added cruelly:-

Go and make your peace elsewhere with your friends – if you've got any. I can't do with it. Shut up. I don't want to see you. You know how to get someone in a stew. I can do without you now. You've come to nose around but you're wasting your time.

Inexplicably, despite that nasty outburst, I was invited back that evening for a drink when my Aunty Ruth turned up. Things were not so bad - until my brother phoned. I could hear my mother saying that everything was okay, but then things then turned nasty again when she started talking again about 'Eileen's money'. My aunt left hurriedly, scurrying off like a frightened rabbit.

I visited Mother again and she returned jewellery which I had given to her as gifts some time previously. She seemed okay initially but then got angry again for no apparent reason. Her comments, again hurtful, included:-

Don't come round tomorrow. There's no point in staying. I asked you ages ago to sort it out and you didn't. The flat is Michael's. You've got something sly going on in your mind! You didn't contact Eileen, did you? What about the nephew and niece? What did they do for her? Go and do some more snooping! You transferred £54,000 into your own bank account!

This was the first I had heard of the figure of £54,000. I didn't go to see Mother again as it seemed pointless, but I went to see her solicitor. He was a Mason and appeared very pleasant, to begin with at least. He promised to keep an eye on my mother and to make sure no-one took advantage of her.

While there I told the lawyer Mother would probably be moving to the Masonic Home in Devon and he felt this would not be a good move. Mother had lived in Bridlington all her life and had many friends there who visited her.

I then visited Iain Bryce. He was a past Deputy Grand Master in the Masons, and supposed to be a family friend, although Mother had told me he never visited. He and his wife were busy at the time so an arrangement was made for me to visit the next day, although his wife, Janet, would be out. On reflection I thought it would be nice to see her too. So I telephoned to rearrange my visit. I was not prepared for the verbal abuse that followed. Iain had obviously phoned Mother, who had said she did not want him to see me. It was obvious Iain had also listened to stories from my brother by launching into a pretty vicious attack, warning me that I might find myself cut out of other peoples' wills too. I was astounded and saw no point in continuing with the conversation so I ended it. If Iain had listened to my side of the story he might not have found it at all astounding that my father should wish to financially help his daughter and her family. I am sure Ian Bryce's daughters have benefited from his financial assistance. I would have hoped so as one is a single mother.

While in England I visited Social Services and conveyed my fears about the well-being of my mother. The staff was sympathetic initially and said they would check up on her, as well as suggesting other agencies which might be able to help.

Despite Mother stating I had no friends in Bridlington, I actually did and while in my old home town I visited a number of them. I enjoyed my stay in the bed and breakfast and visited an elderly family friend in a nursing home. She invited me to return to the home for lunch the next day when her daughter would be visiting. Ian and I had entertained this lady's granddaughter in New Zealand and occasionally see her in Sydney where she now lives with her child. I also visited an old school friend, then two neighbours of Mother's, including a doctor who lived next door.

While in England I also phoned my brother. He greeted me sharply, in a business-like manner. I opened the conversation:-

Adrienne: How are you?
Michael: Fine thank you.
Adrienne: I think there's a few things we need to talk about aren't there?
Michael: If you want to.
Adrienne: First of all I was a bit disappointed how Mother was at my meeting. I find her mentally confused.
Michael: Yes.
Adrienne: I thought it would be a good idea to have Social Services

call around to see if there's anything they can help her with? Do you think that would be a good idea?

Michael: I wouldn't have thought so.

Adrienne: Why not?

Michael: Because I don't think she is mentally confused. I have had a longer relationship with her over weeks, months and years, and I assess the situation on a regular basis. What do you suppose Social Services would interest themselves in?

Adrienne: Maybe to get more help in the house. Age Concern might also be able to help with a visitor to pop in and see her, perhaps more visitors on occasions.

Michael: She has visitors. She has home help.

Adrienne: Well maybe there are other things. What's the matter with asking?

Michael: Because I discuss it with her on a daily basis and she has everything she needs.

Adrienne: Okay, let's move on to Eileen then. You saw fit not to tell me that Eileen had died.

Michael snapped at this point, seemingly a little embarrassed that I was raising the issue of our step-mother, as he knew what was coming next:-

Michael: For what reason? You haven't had contact with her for seven years!

Adrienne: I think there are finances to discuss aren't there?

Michael: I don't think so.

Adrienne: Did you not find the bank account in Jersey?

Michael: Yes.

Adrienne: You found it?

Michael: Yes and I also found that you drafted a letter making it a joint account dated 29th August 1989, a month after our father's death – in your handwriting!

[The draft was produced to me at a later date and was actually dated 30th September 1989, two months after my father's death and only six months before Eileen closed the Jersey account, according to her diary.

A copy of this draft letter appears as an appendix].

Adrienne: Okay. I would be pleased to see it.

Michael: You don't need to.

Adrienne: I do need to because I must have completely forgotten about it and I have no knowledge of it, if there's a bank account. So whose name is it in?

Michael: Tough!

Adrienne: I didn't catch that?

Michael: Tough.

Adrienne: Tough? Oh. Okay. I presume you are the executor of Eileen's will?

Michael: You can presume what you like.

Adrienne: I presume you had power of attorney for her?

Michael: Again you can presume what you like?

Adrienne: I presume you registered the power of attorney with the Court of Protection?

Michael: Again you can presume what you like.

Adrienne: I presume that you also advised relatives you had registered it with the Court of Protection?

Michael: Again you can presume.

Adrienne: And the witnesses to the Deed of Transfer of her flat?

Michael: Again you can presume what you like. None of this is any of your business.

Adrienne: I think it is when it comes down to Mother and for what you've done to Eileen.

Michael: I don't think so.

Adrienne: Would you please send a copy of the will and probate to my solicitor?

Michael: No.

Adrienne: Okay I think we'll terminate the conversation now and I'll take matters forward. Okay? So much for the conversation we were to have.

Michael: None of this is your business, Adrienne, to do with Eileen. You terminated with Eileen a long time ago. (Conveniently forgetting I had been ordered to terminate my relationship.) I have looked after her, so you have no right whatsoever to investigate anything at this stage. Everything has been finished, done and dealt with. Officially!

Adrienne: I have found out what you have done to Eileen and I think you are going to do the same with my mother.

Michael snapped again, this time with more vehemence:-

What you did to Eileen! You took her money and you would have taken Mother's money as well

I then had my say and it was short and to the point:-

Don't be ridiculous. Conversation terminates now.

On my return to New Zealand I continued with my investigations into Michael and his transactions and dealings with Eileen. I don't know if it was the conversations I had had in England or not, but somehow, my resilience seemed to have been replenished!

~ *Twenty Five* ~

I wrote to my mother's solicitor, David Burnett of Messrs Stuart Smith and Burnett, confirming I had met with him and I wished to put my fears about my mother on record. I also repeated my thought that I believed the intervention of Social Services would be a good idea as I was really worried about Mother.

I also I wrote to Mother, setting out my fears and advising I wished Social Services to keep an eye on her and assist where possible. The response came not from her, but from her solicitor and it constituted quite a change of direction from our discussion in his office in Bridlington.

He stated my mother didn't want to hear from me or Rachel again and if I contacted her, it would constitute harassment – in his opinion. Poor Rachel, what had she done? Perhaps it was because she had warned me Michael was in Bridlington, which caused me to wait until he had departed before I visited Mother. Shortly after my letter arrived, Rachel received a similar one from the solicitor, effectively telling her not to contact her grandmother. Rachel had always had an arrangement to ring her granny on a certain day every month and the letter therefore came as a big shock to her.

Despite being instructed not to make contact, I continued to telephone Mother. In September 2009 she wrote to me herself. This letter stated:

This has gone on long enough, the phone calls to me when you have been asked to stop by my solicitor and the harassment to Michael, over Eileen's will which was made legally and above board, and there is nothing you can do about it. Her signature was witnessed by two very responsible people. What do you expect? Not being mentioned, having deceived her out of £50,000, leaving Michael to fend for her needs for seven years. Michael and Penny have just returned from a holiday in New Zealand and say what a beautiful country it is. Get on with your life, leave us alone and enjoy your country. Incidentally I am of sound mind and have not included either you or Rachel in my will. Your Mother.

I knew that Michael and Penny had been to New Zealand as I had received a postcard from Auckland which advised:

Nice house. Neighbours seem pleasant too. Good write-up on Taupo in today's New Zealand Herald. Had intended to call to resolve Mother but see no need to intrude on your privacy so long as you do not intrude on mine. Mother says you tried to phone again. You've had a letter from her solicitor, don't make matters worse.

Michael didn't even sign the postcard but I knew his handwriting. It appeared he had sat outside my house and then talked to my neighbours. Was it intended to frighten me I wondered? If he had really wanted to resolve matters why did he not simply knock on the door?

But no matter the intention, the clever psychology of my battle-hardened brother was working, with my nightmares turning into horrendous visions of him murdering me.

I had also been told my brother was reporting me to Humberside Police for allegedly harassing my mother. So I wrote to that Police force, welcoming their intervention and again setting the record straight. I advised that any investigating officers could get hold of me expediently by telephone. Of course, they didn't.

Mother's solicitor had also written to Bridlington Police and later I was given a copy of his letter in which Mr Burnett outlined the story – from my brother's point of view. In that letter to the Police, the solicitor also stated I had visited him in Bridlington but he had told me he was not prepared to discuss Mother. This is untrue.

He overlooked the fact I held her original power of attorney which has been drawn up by him. He also stated I had contacted Social Services. This is correct. But he went on to indicate I felt my mother was unable to look after herself and therefore should be removed to a care home, which was incorrect. We had discussed the fact the care home option would be wrong in her circumstances, particularly if she had to go to Exeter. I had actually asked Social Services to arrange the intervention of Age Concern, simply to see if a regular visitor could call on her.

My defence against harassment, as always, was that I felt a crime had been committed, but not by me. I really believed my brother was psychologically abusing our mother.

I also contacted Social Services again, making a complaint in the context that this agency had not acted in the best interests of Mother. I felt there was a duty, at least, to investigate my concerns.

Social Services initially advised I could not make a complaint because I was not a 'service user', or at least I should have had written permission from Mother to make a complaint on her behalf. This was hardly going to happen, unless she was prepared to stand against Michael, but I persisted. Having been told to contact customer services, I sent off a number of emails but was eventually told to stop - unless I had physical evidence of abuse.

I continued sending my mother postcards, and Mr Burnett continued writing to the Police.

In December 2009 Mr Burnett wrote to my mother, a copy of which was given to me much later, stating:-

At long last your daughter is being served with another harassment notice. I am convinced from the way she has acted she has mental problems.

I was visited again by Police in New Zealand. They were very apologetic in disturbing and upsetting me, but again pointed out they simply had a duty to investigate alleged harassment of Mother by me. The visit came to nothing – certainly no harassment notices were served upon me.

It was also interesting to note that as well as detectives, the community officer called on me. He indicated the Police had received a letter from my sister-in-law, Penny Lobb, asking if harassment orders had been served on me. Again he was very sympathetic to my cause, saying he should really write back indicating that information would have been confidential, but I gave my full permission to reply confirming no harassment orders had ever been issued and served against me.

In the meantime, my complaint against the East Riding of Yorkshire Social Services progressed. This was based on a customer services adviser telling me I should lodge a formal complaint with the local council's chief executive, Nigel Pearson. If I remained unsatisfied after that process I could then go to the Ombudsman.

As events unfolded, I was unsatisfied by my treatment and so I did indeed seek the intervention of the Ombudsman. The substance of my new complaint was that my mother should be interviewed without my brother being present, and she should be specifically asked what had caused her hatred towards my daughter and me. I felt also she should specifically be questioned to find out precisely what she had been told about my step-mother's finances by my brother.

My complaint against the East Riding of Yorkshire Social Services was not upheld, which did not surprise me either. But what was surprising was that this agency served a section 32 (3) Notice under the 1974 Local Government Act, meaning I could not see the reasoning behind that decision. I wrote to the council's chief executive asking why I had not been informed of this official statutory censure before, but never received a satisfactory response.

With that complaint effectively over, my other lines of enquiry continued. My solicitors in Warminster wrote to the firm of solicitors in Northampton who had acted for my brother in property matters in the past. There was no reply.

My solicitors then wrote to my brother direct, asking for specific details of the circumstances surrounding Eileen's death and the transfer of her apartment. I had already managed to obtain a copy of the title of her property. My solicitor also asked for details of the Jersey Bank account which my brother stated he had found and he asked the whereabouts of her jewellery and possessions. But there was no reply from my brother.

However, I continued phoning around, and my perseverance paid off. I actually traced Eileen's 1990 will naming me as executor and the 1999 codicil to Scott Bailey, solicitors in Lymington.

My find really enabled me to continue with my enquiries. If I had not found a will in my favour, this could have been the end of the story. I would not have had any right to challenge a will, as I was not a blood relation. So I ended up in the clutches of Nick Jutton, the head of litigation with Scott Bailey solicitors.

~ *Twenty Six* ~

As it was to develop, my relationship with Nick was a long and unhappy one. I had no wish to go to litigation and failed to see how I ended up with Nick acting for me. A partner, Ian Davies, drew up the will and if I had been unable to act as the executor, he was named. I expected Ian Davies to get involved, but he did not.

However Nick did write to my brother on 30th September 2008 advising that the last will of Eileen's known to their firm, and therefore me, was one naming me as an executor. This had the effect of bringing my brother out of the woodwork - he replied the next day, indicating three wills had been made after the 1990 one. Michael also suggested Nick Jutton should contact Hampshire Constabulary and the New Forest District Council in 'respect of his sister's behaviour'.

My brother met Nick ten days later and at that meeting he produced three different wills. Nick subsequently told me -

The wills were dated 28th June 2001, 3rd March 2002 and 21st September 2007 and they all appoint your brother as executor. All of them left your step-mother's estate to your brother, although the first two made several minor pecuniary legacies. The last will was signed by your step-mother while she was resident in the Belmore Lodge Nursing Home. The wills carried the names of two witnesses, your brother's mother-in-law, Olive Skae and the late Douggie Croshawe. The address for Mrs Skae was in Lymington.

My brother would not let Nick have copies of the wills, nor would he discuss the transfer of the apartment. That was a clever move, because unfortunately I did not realise Nick Jutton was incapable of copying information correctly so it was to cost me dearly in time and money.

My brother stated at that meeting Eileen had a bank account in Jersey in which the proceeds of the apartment in Spain were held. He also indicated I had drafted a letter to make the account joint with Eileen, then I allegedly transferred the entire proceeds of £54,000 into my own NatWest bank account. This – according to my brother – is what had caused the falling out between Eileen and me. Both Nick Jutton and I had difficulty with the time frame involved as ten years had elapsed since I allegedly took the money from the Jersey bank, during which time there were no problems in the relationship I had with Eileen.

Nick then suggested we trace Olive Skae and we try to obtain Eileen's medical records. We were successful in both. We also contacted the Matron at Belmore Lodge Nursing Home and Nick wrote again to my brother asking for copies of all the wills. My enthusiastic new solicitor suggested we get statements from members of Eileen's family since they were also highly suspicious of my brother's actions.

Michael responded to the letter from Nick again refusing to produce copies of the wills. He also indicated the transfer of the apartment was irrelevant as it did not form part of Eileen's estate. He stated as the three wills superseded the one I had, he would not provide any further information, and insisted I had no right of interest in my step-mother's estate. Nick wrote again to my brother on 7th November, indicating I had very real concerns over the validity of the wills and again asked him to produce them. Once again, Michael refused to do so.

Firmly believing a criminal offence had taken place, I also instructed Nick to report the matter to Hampshire Police. The response from the Police was predictable with the advice being furnished that action should be taken through the Civil Court.

Nick's next move was that I should issue a subpoena to lodge a will and this I did, requiring the three wills dated 28th June 2001, 3rd March 2002 and 21st September 2007 be produced. The process server frustratingly took weeks to serve that subpoena, finding my elusive brother was either away or out.

Eventually, on 2nd March 2009, my brother responded, asserting that he took great exception to the behaviour of the process server. According to Michael, he had been away and his wife was home alone in an isolated house. By this stage Michael and Penny had moved from Pattishall to Winkleigh, a small village near Exeter.

Despite that complaint, my solicitor finally received copies of two wills, those dated the 21st September 2007 and 28th June 2001. There was no reference to the third will. As I was to find out later, Nick had written the date of the third will down incorrectly and therefore the date was incorrect on the subpoena.

On receiving a copy of the will of 21st September 2007 I found it had not been witnessed by Mrs Skae but by a lady living in Lymington

– another error by Nick Jutton.

Subsequently Nick wrote to this lady, who was not best pleased in being contacted, but she stated she was merely visiting her mother at Belmore Nursing Home when the Matron approached her asking her to witness a resident's signature as staff members were forbidden to do this. She described the scene, and it would appear my brother was present as was Douggie Croshawe, the other witness.

Lengthy correspondence followed but my solicitor eventually received a letter from my brother producing a copy of a will dated 8th of November 1999. Michael confirmed this will was made less than three months after my argument with Eileen. Its format showed it was effectively what one might call a self-help will, having been written and witnessed without any solicitor giving independent advice.

My brother then reported Nick Jutton to the Solicitors Regulation Authority. His complaint was that my solicitor had acted in an unprofessional manner by using me 'presumably for the purpose of incurring costs.' In that complaint Michael described me as a 'very vulnerable person who, in recent years, has shown increasingly delusional tendencies.'

Michael also indicated he could not allow me to be used by Nick Jutton, indicating at the same time that his law firm had used me – 'a particularly sad and vulnerable pensioner' – as a source of income in a difficult period for business. This complaint was, of course, not upheld after an investigation.

I then wrote to Olive Skae asking for details of the witnessing of the transfer, only to receive a short, curt typewritten reply. 'I refer to your impertinent letter of 7th July 2009 and advise you that a copy of this had been lodged with the Police. Do not contact me again.'

Three days later another letter, typewritten in a layout not dissimilar to that received from Mrs Skae, was sent to our friend Mike at his Romsey address. This read:-

On 7th July a letter written by Mrs Adrienne Nairn addressed to my 88 year old mother, Mrs O M Skae, was posted in Southampton. The letter was distressing and has been passed to the Police. I inform you of this so that you are aware of the situation and apologise for bothering you in the event that you know nothing of this letter.

This letter is signed by Penny Lobb, Michael's wife and the daughter of Olive Skae. It was a strange letter to write to a complete stranger. Fortunately Mike, our good friend, took it all in his stride and passed it on to me immediately. My letter to Mrs Skae was not distressing, as attested by my solicitor. It was polite and merely asked for information. But the response can be seen as proof that Penny Lobb was not adverse to making allegations against me by writing to strangers.

By this time Nick Jutton had decided Counsel advice was required and, admitting he had made mistakes with dates and witness details, he could contact a friend, Derek Marshall, a barrister, in a personal capacity. He did so, but Derek Marshall advised he would need proper instruction. This we did, but not very satisfactorily. I specified questions I wanted answered by Counsel, but Nick didn't include them in his brief and that makes a big difference. It appears if any point is not raised specifically by the instructing solicitor, no matter how obvious, this will not be considered in coming to a conclusion as far as the law is concerned. On the basis of what he had been told, Derek Marshall advised that in his view I did not have much chance of success. So while I ended up paying a large invoice, I still did not get answers to the questions I had asked.

We entered 2010, a new year, and I specifically instructed my solicitor to go ahead and take my brother to Court. After digging up so much evidence, I wanted to take this action to prove what I had known was the truth from the start. When Nick Jutton did not do as I asked. I began to lose my temper.

Eventually Nick claimed it appeared there was a breakdown in his client relationship, and he refused to act for me any more in the circumstances. The issue then was what to do next. I could have given up, but I am not a person who does so easily. So I stuck a pin in a book and came up with Tony Cockayne of Michelmores in Exeter, a choice that, regrettably, turned out to be another bad one.

~ *Twenty Seven* ~

However before I relate that sorry saga we have to go back to my perseverance in my on-going investigations. During this period I discovered my brother's solicitors, Messrs Edward St John Smyth of Northants, had prepared various wills for my stepmother. I felt strongly that my stepmother should have had independent legal advice, most certainly before she gave all of the equitable value of her penthouse apartment to Michael, allegedly for repaying our deceased father's debts.

I had also discovered that Eileen had dealt with Scott Bailey, solicitors in Lymington, over a period of about ten years. She went to them on her own, unbeknown to me at the time and received all the advice she needed. So the question arose, why would she suddenly use an entirely different legal firm in Northampton?

In January 2009, I reported Edward St J Smyth to the Solicitors Regulation Authority. The subsequent investigation took months, but eventually the SRA discovered Ray Wood of that law firm prepared the will dated 21st of September 2007, while Edward St John Smyth prepared the will dated the 28th of June 2001. The law firm informed the SRA there was no will dated the third of March 2002, but there was an earlier one dated the 3rd of March 2000, which had not been prepared by them. At long last maybe I had the date of the elusive third will which my brother had originally waved in front of Nick Jutton?

However, when confronted with this information my brother responded by indicating he had no knowledge of any will dated 3rd of March 2000 and asked where we got this information. When we eventually obtained a copy of this will, we found it was dated in my brother's hand, on the same date as the deed of gift of Eileen's apartment, where the date was also written by Michael.

The SRA found my step-mother didn't seek independent advice or instruct Edward St J Smyth regarding the power of attorney either. Many letters and emails went backwards and forwards, but that authority eventually delivered its decision on 16th October 2009.

The SRA's formal findings were:-

That Edward St J Smyth had acted in breach of Rule 1(c) of the Solicitors' Practice Rules 1990 and further, that he had acted in breach of Principle 12.05 of The Guide to the Professional Conduct of Solicitors 1999 (8th Edition).

It further found:-

That Raymond Wood had acted in breach of Rule 1(c) of the Solicitors' Practice Rules 1990 and further that he had acted in breach of principle 12.05 of The Guide to the Professional Conduct of Solicitors 1999 (8th Edition) and that Raymond Wood had acted in breach of Rule 1(d) Solicitors' Practice Rules 1990.

The SRA stated its reasons and made the following comments:-

In 2001 Mrs [Eileen] Lobb wrote to Mr Smyth asking him to make a new will for her. The letter was typed and she had signed it at the end. It provided for a number of specific legacies to a wide variety of people and was very clear. Mr Smyth sent her a draft which was written in accordance with the instructions but Mrs Lobb was clearly unhappy with it and she returned the draft significantly amended. She deleted beneficiaries. Mrs Lobb sent back the new will but the finished article was significantly different from the original draft. The Adjudicator was concerned that Mr St. J Smyth did not express concern at the significant differences in Mrs Lobb's apparent wishes between her original letter and the draft he sent her within a matter of a few weeks. The principle then applicable was 12.05 which clearly stated 'where instructions are received from third parties, solicitors should obtain written instructions from the client that he or she wishes the solicitor to act. In any case of doubt the solicitor should see the client or take other appropriate steps to confirm instructions'.

The Adjudicator also stated that although there were letters from Mrs Lobb, the solicitor did not know her - although he knew her step-son - and he should have taken the additional step to ensure that what Mrs Lobb was asking him to do was what Mrs Lobb herself actually wanted him to do. He found that Mr St. J Smyth did not act in Mrs Lobb's best interests. Mr Wood was involved in two further transactions. In 2006 he was asked to register and put into legal effect the assignment by way of gift which Mrs Lobb had executed in 2000. His instructions came not from Mrs Lobb but from her step-son, Michael Lobb, presumably under the terms of the power of attorney which Mrs Lobb had executed in 1999. The Adjudicator stated Mr Wood should have checked the position to make quite certain the deed of gift was what Mrs Lobb wanted. A client care letter was sent to Mrs Lobb by Mr Wood and it was returned signed by her step-son. Mr Wood should have made personal contact with Mrs Lobb to satisfy himself as to the position. Thereafter there was a further request for a new will made by Mrs Lobb in 2007. The client care letter was sent to her and was returned, again signed not by Mrs Lobb but by Michael Lobb. The Adjudicator then recorded:-

> A draft will was then prepared and sent to Mr [Michael] Lobb which he himself returned, endorsed by his step-mother 'in accordance with her wishes'. There are the written words 'I approve this draft Eileen M Lobb' at the foot of page one but no such signature at the foot of page two. The draft was executed and Mr Lobb paid the bill for his step-mother's will. Mr Wood should certainly have taken a step to check that the instructions given on behalf of Mrs Lobb were indeed what she wanted. Both Mr St. J. Smyth and Raymond Wood were warned as to their professional conduct.

All this was of course was very helpful and to me the Solicitors Regulations Authority was the only body to have actually done its job properly. However, what was the outcome? The solicitors involved got a 'slap over the wrists' and were told not to do it again. In the meantime my brother had got away with a penthouse apartment valued at around £600,000. I believe, on those grounds, I clearly would have won the civil action against my brother if Nick Jutton had instructed Counsel fully and correctly.

Before being able to go to the Legal Ombudsman, I was required to make a complaint about Nick Jutton to his own law firm, but I knew I would not get far on that front. My complaint went to the head of customer complaints, who was Nick Jutton himself, no less. However I went through the process anyway, with the thrust of my complaint being:-

> i. That Nick Jutton did not carry out my instruction, which was to initiate legal proceedings against my brother.

The reply was that Nick did not think legal proceedings would be in my best interests and the members of his firm agreed with him. My complaint on that front was not upheld.

ii. That the delays had been unreasonable. The fact that I had sent numerous emails to Nick asking for a reply was disregarded.
I was advised Nick did have to have major surgery at one stage and I should have been informed that there would be a delay for that reason. This complaint was not upheld.

iii. That Nick gave me incorrect information - that he told me Mrs Skae was a witness to the 2007 will when she was not.
His firm stated that Nick stood by the attendance note he made that Mrs Skae was a witness and he could not explain why, when the will was produced, another person was the witness. Nick also stood by his assertion that he saw a will dated March 2002, although the will dated March 2000 was later produced. But the firm could not conclude that Nick had made a mistake, saying it had no doubt that his report of the meeting with Michael was accurate, notwithstanding the fact of my brother's subsequent denials. This complaint was not upheld.

iv. That there was a failure to reply to letters.
This complaint was not upheld although I gave numerous examples of times I had to write requesting replies to my emails.

v. That I had been caused excessive distress and inconvenience.
I should have thought this was obvious as Nick had ultimately refused to continue with my case, therefore leaving me without a solicitor at a crucial time. But this complaint was not upheld either.

I wrote a lengthy reply to this report, but the case worker was not going to change their mind. I was however invited to take the case to the Legal Services Ombudsman, which, of course, I did, again to no avail.
The Ombudsman process took about a year and I was no further forward in having my claim against my brother and his actions in relation to Eileen's property resolved.
Since my relationship with Nick Jutton had broken down, I decided to consider the involvement of appointed counsel Derek Marshall. His original assessment had been founded on facts as they pertained before

the Solicitors Regulation Authority found against Messrs Edward St Smyth and I felt its decision may have changed his thoughts.

I decided to write and make a complaint, specifically indicating he had not answered twelve points I had raised, on which I required answers.

The reply was that a barrister's instructions must come from the instructing solicitor, not the client of the solicitor. However, the only question posed by Mr Jutton was whether there were grounds to challenge Eileen Lobb's last will, or indeed any earlier wills? That was what Mr Marshall based his advice on.

Mr Jutton had in fact enclosed a copy of my email detailing my questions but because they were not in his instructions, Mr Marshall did not consider them.

For his part, Mr Jutton suggested I should have checked the instructions which went to the barrister and I should have made sure the questions raised by me were included. I made the point that the reason I went to solicitors was to ensure things were done in line with the law. How was I to know Mr Marshall would not consider my questions in the accompanying email? But there it was, the complaint against Mr Marshall was not upheld either. A familiar trend was developing.

The Bar Standards Board, which was then asked to review the situation, didn't provide any solace either.

In hindsight, I now know I should have lodged another complaint against Nick Jutton, but it was much too late. There does come a time when more important things loom but by then I had no faith in the process, particularly in the context that the facts of the case at issue are not considered.

~ *Twenty Eight* ~

Throughout all this I did have one ally – Ted Farmer, Eileen's first cousin. I had previously tried to get Ted to intervene in the ridiculous row with Eileen, telling him she could be in serious trouble with the authorities if she persisted in telling different stories about her Jersey bank account to different public authorities, but I heard no more from him about that matter.

When I discovered Eileen had died, I wondered if Ted's children had received anything from her estate as she had been very fond of his son, young Teddy, and his twin sisters, Alison and Susan. They had featured in her 1990 will by way of pecuniary bequests.

Ted was to prove very helpful in my investigations over the years, but he was no match for my brother. Ted provided some background on his family and the aftermath of the death of his cousin:-

Eileen Lobb and I were first cousins. Our mothers were sisters and were quite close. There was deep mutual affection between Eileen and our three children (twin daughters and a son, now adult) from their birth, she having no (surviving) children of her own. To them she was always Auntie Eileen. I was very disappointed to learn they were apparently not mentioned in her will. However after Eileen's death both Adrienne and another cousin, Olive, quite independently asked if our children had received legacies. From conversations with Eileen, it was clear our children were to be beneficiaries. Olive used the word 'substantial' and further said our daughters were also to receive her jewellery, including two good engagement rings, one each. I now know that during a car journey to bring Eileen up here for one of a number of Christmases she spent with us, she told my son-in-law, Mark (of whom she was also very fond) of her intentions.

Ted also provided a summary of Eileen's last year of life – 2007. He and his wife, Janet, had visited her that year. He indicated his wife and both daughters are radiographers not doctors, but had experience of patients and medical staff in hospital environments. During the week commencing 28th May, Ted had a phone call from Douggie Croshawe, who said Eileen had an injury from a fall in her flat and was therefore in Southampton General Hospital. There was no immediate cause for concern, so their first visit was on 10th July.

Ted and Janet found Eileen to be fairly normal, all things considered, but noted her swollen ankles, indicative of heart failure. Eileen got confused between the family names too. She was up and walking, but was looking forward to being discharged from hospital.

Douggie was planning for her to go to his flat where he could provide a room, but on 13th July he advised Ted and Janet that Eileen was then being transferred to Fordingbridge Hospital for convalescence prior to discharge. Her stay at Fordingbridge was brief. She suffered breathlessness and panic attacks so she was returned to Southampton General.

Ted later recalled:-

As her physical health weakened, her mental health declined. She became rather confused and took less interest in conversation. It is fair to question whether she could appreciate the full implications of matters such as signing legal documents, or could be bothered. I understand Michael Lobb held power of attorney and she was very vulnerable. Douggie Croshawe, aged 95, was an obvious but unfortunate choice of witness to the transfer document, but is regrettably no longer able to explain the circumstances.

Ted visited Eileen again on 14th August and found significant deterioration. Ted found conversation with his cousin difficult. Both she and Douggie had been upset by a visit from my brother Michael. At one point Douggie proclaimed: 'After all this I shall not have him to stay at my place again and not cook him bacon and eggs. He can doss down in Eileen's place'. Janet was surprised by the outburst about Michael and although she wanted to dig for more detail, she felt it inappropriate to probe.

Eileen was moved to Hythe Hospital and then to Belmore Lodge on 5th September.

Ted observed when he visited Eileen on 25th September that her condition had deteriorated further. She was having panic attacks and was fitted with oxygen tubes. Conversation was difficult and her attention span was very short. He thought Eileen had realised any hope of returning home was gone. Michael had been down for a week with his wife, Penny, and her mother.

Ted and Janet continued to get phone reports from Douggie and made a visit on 28th November. They found Eileen very much deteriorated, with very little ability to converse, and assessed she had no fight left in her. Douggie was very tetchy about Michael's activities but did not elaborate in front of other visitors.

Ted went on to advise that after Eileen died, Douggie had told him there would be a gathering at the hotel in the village after the funeral. Michael disagreed and changed this to Eileen's apartment, which was not to everyone's approval.

Michael asked Ted and Janet if there was anything they particularly wanted but they said they would have considered it extremely offensive and unacceptable to walk around and pick up mementoes at that time in the presence of fifty other people!

Michael and Penny seemed not to be part of that gathering, removed and distant appearing anxious for people to go as soon as possible. Michael declined to open another bottle of wine to replenish Janet's glass.

Ted says of that gathering:-

As we were departing Dawn, Eileen's niece, spoke to us in the car park. She then wrote to me on 10th January as though I was dealing with Eileen's affairs, requesting photographs and anything connected with her mother, Vera [Eileen's sister]. She also wished to know where Eileen's ashes were to be placed to pay her respects. Alison accompanied me to represent my family at Douggie Croshawe's funeral on 16th June and asked Michael about Eileen's ashes. He led the way through the grounds of the crematorium to a tree, waved an arm and said 'they are about here, they should be good for the tree.' This was a cold and callous remark in very bad taste which caused some loss of composure. It was questionable behaviour of a supposed supportive and affectionate step-son. There is no name or memorial to mark the place as there are for thousands of others in the grounds.

My brother had inferred to my solicitor, Nick Jutton, that the 'Farmers had been taken care of'. Ted took exception to this, and the fact that he was supposed to know the reason for the transfer of Eileen's apartment to Michael. Ted told me later:-

Michael came here on 31st March 2008 and handed over some

costume jewellery and souvenirs of very little value to pass on to my daughters. This cannot be all Eileen's jewellery as there were no rings, as specifically mentioned by Olive. He mentioned he had funded a new boiler in Eileen's apartment, that her estate was less than £5000, it did not need to go for probate and he was sole beneficiary. I have to admit to surprise and did not question him. He declined any refreshment and was anxious to leave. We have since discovered Eileen's apartment was transferred to Michael on 24th July 2007, two months after her admission to hospital and five months before her death, apparently for no payment.

An estate agent in Milford quite familiar with Richmond Court informed me that even in the current turbulent market it would make £600,000. We have been thinking more about the possible pressures. I suspect Michael would be trained in psychological techniques. My wife and I have discussed this matter with a local solicitor who considers it very suspicious.

Early this year we received by post a package containing a gold watch and a note from Douggie Croshawe saying Eileen made him promise to give it to Alison.

Alison reflected on one visit to Eileen, advising me:-

> I asked Douggie if Michael had visited again. I was within earshot of Auntie Eileen. Douggie replied that he had, but his reply was in a most bitter manner, through gritted teeth. He implied Michael's visit had not been agreeable to Eileen at all. Both Douggie and Auntie Eileen were most put out by the mention of his name.

I have had lengthy correspondence with Ted Farmer. He is incensed at the situation, having been led to believe his three children would have inherited something of value from Eileen. He describes events as 'a well-executed and ruthless plan, as one would expect from your brother.'

Ted also relates a conversation with a neighbour in Richmond Court who became very friendly with Douggie and Eileen. He knew of the transfer of the apartment. This neighbour advised that Michael had told him our father, Maurice, had willed the apartment to Eileen for her life - or as long as she wished to live there - at which time it would pass to Michael himself. I believe this is blatantly untrue as my father did not leave a will, as far as I knew, and the apartment was never registered in his name. We also know Eileen gifted the apartment to Michael in 2000.

I have often wondered if Eileen had actually understood the implications of the deed of gift, which didn't contain a clause specifying she could live there rent free. I also wondered about the delay in registering the title with the Land Registry. I had been told it was an oversight but I suspect my brother didn't want the matter publicly known - particularly by members of the committee of Richmond Court Ltd, who might have questioned it.

I do not find it surprising that Eileen became angry after Michael told her he had registered the legal title with Land Registry in 2007 – with no condition she could continue to live there rent free.

In January 2009 Ted Farmer received a confusing phone call from Michael in relation to the various wills and beneficiaries. The comment that one will provided for the twins but excluded young Ted was particularly upsetting to him. I was to find out why the following year.

Michael had been keen to give his own credentials to Ted during that phone call and it went something like this – a soldier twenty five years, decorated four times for gallantry, had paid off his father's debts, had paid for repairs to Eileen's patio doors cost £1800 and service charges of £1600 a year, and had provided for some of her holidays, and so on. But he still refused to provide copies of the wills, even to Ted.

Ted also notes he questioned the issue of the jewellery and was assured he had been given all that remained. Michael claimed Eileen sold jewellery to raise cash – at very low prices – but conceded she would not have sold her engagement rings.

Five minutes after that call ended, Michael phoned again to say his wife had reminded him that the rings had been stolen by 'immigrant' carers who had come in to dress Eileen's leg ulcers. Ted asked if this theft had been investigated. He was also told Eileen's estate was less than £3500 with the funeral cost being £2600.

Michael went on to advise Ted that her furniture and effects were sent to auction raising about £150. Ted considered this to be dreadful and reminded Michael of the understanding that after the funeral, a visit was to be arranged later to see what the relatives would like to keep. Michael retorted that Ted should have told him of that desire.

Following the communications from Ted Farmer, I remembered we had taken a video of all Eileen's possessions for insurance purposes. Eileen obviously believed she had precious items to protect at that time. I still have the video and having viewed it reminded Ted of many items.

He subsequently observed: 'It beggars belief. Now we are reminded of many of those treasures. Compare that list with the box of trinkets here which I have not had the heart even to show the twins and what fetched £150 at auction. Could she really have sold so much? We are horrified.'

In my view, Eileen should not have needed to sell anything. Considering the gift of the apartment, my brother should have paid all Eileen's expenses willingly, as I had done for the ten years between 1989 and 1999.

Ted has also related the thrust of yet another 'acrimonious phone call' from Michael, who had discovered that I had consequently reported the 'theft' of the rings to the Police and quite rightly assumed Ted had told me.

Ted revealed Michael had said in this call that Eileen did not want the theft reported for fear of retribution and indicated she had no personal possessions insurance. I found this very strange because holding her power of attorney he should have made sure she was covered. Ted also pointed out that was stupid.

Michael responded by saying that if the engagement rings had not been stolen they would be still in Eileen's estate and thus would become his property. Personally, I knew Eileen was insured because an item was stolen from her front door and I had to help her claim the insurance monies, hence the decision to make the video of all her possessions. There was also a reference in her diary that she needed to sort out her household insurance because she had been 'paying twice'.

Ted also wanted to raise the state of anger and tension from both Eileen and Douggie which members of his family had found on their visits to them.

Michael admitted he and Eileen did not always agree but insisted he always spoke from the heart in Eileen's best interests. The transfer of the apartment may not have been viewed in this light by Eileen herself, but it seems she had no choice but to go along with it.

Ted Farmer today remains a staunch ally, one who has the strong conviction that Michael manipulated Eileen and took ownership of the apartment, and all her possessions, to quench his own greed.

In an email dated 19th June 2009 Ted observed that the 1999 will appeared to be a do-it-yourself job – one created just four months after a professionally-drafted document - in which ten people fell right out of favour.

In successive wills there appear to be inexplicable discrepancies.

Only in the event Michael predeceased her, are Alison and Susan Farmer mentioned. Their address quoted is Ted Farmer's address whereas they are both married and have their own homes. Eileen would have known their married names and addresses. William Tate, Eileen's brother-in-law, is mentioned in a typewritten unsigned instruction allegedly by her dated 7th February 2007 to Messrs Edwards St J Smyth, the law firm drafting her will. However William Tate died in 2001 and Eileen went to his funeral!

I now wonder if heavy pressure was brought to bear not to distribute assets but concentrate on a sole beneficiary – maybe in exchange for some degree of financial support. Given the on-going behaviour of my own brother, there seem to be valid reasons for believing this was the case.

~ *Twenty Nine* ~

Accusing me of theft, and then going on to tell various people I was a thief and liar had been a particularly callous thing to do and I had considered taking Eileen to Court for defamation. I had actually suggested defamation action to my brother years before and he merely laughed and asked who the Court would believe – me or an old lady with a selective memory?

I did however take legal advice from one of the best legal firms in London specialising in defamation. This law firm charged £2079 for only 11 hours 42 minutes work, which seemed to consist merely of reviewing my papers, taking notes and writing a series of memos between various solicitors within the same building. In the end they came up with the advice that I was 'out of time' – even before concluding whether or not I had a viable case. This costly advice was provided, even though the solicitors had known from the outset when the allegations had originally been made.

However what I found most disconcerting was to come in a letter in which these solicitors suggested it would be tactically to my advantage not to say anything to anyone about seeking legal advice regarding defamation as the one year rule was not generally known. That way, according to them, I could assert pressure with a perceived threat of litigation.

After Eileen's death, the Police became further involved. Ted and I honestly believed some crime had been committed and reported it as such on 4th December 2008 via Nick Jutton, who forwarded my statement to Hampshire Police. In my statement – which was supported by Ted Farmer and my daughter Rachel – I alleged elder abuse, abuse of position, and failure to produce critical documentation.

Detective Inspector Lloyd Tobin of Hampshire Constabulary replied to my solicitor, with the usual get-out clause of there being insufficient evidence to warrant any criminal investigation. However he never contacted me nor questioned me in any way at that stage.

Despite that initial setback I persisted, suggesting that the investigating officer talk directly with Ted Farmer, which he then did.

I am told that this conversation ended abruptly, with the Police officer involved hanging up on Ted.

I reported to Detective Inspector Tobin the theft of two rings, my father's autobiography and of monies from a bank account reportedly held by Eileen. But he merely regurgitated his earlier assessment, leaving many important questions still unanswered.

The fact remained that since my brother didn't register the transfer of the legal title over Eileen's apartment property until 2007, new, compelling and clearly substantial evidence then applied.

This game-changer took the form of a 2004 House of Lords precedent regarding the impecuniosity principle, as my McKenzie friend informed me at a later date.

Before the enactment of that precedent, creditors – including the likes of my brother – were able to claim the whole equitable value of any property owned by debtors in consideration of payment of any debt. That was so even if the value of the property far outweighed the value of the debt. But the effect of the new precedent was if the debtor did not obtain independent legal advice before getting into such debt, creditors could no longer claim the full equitable value if the debtor's sacrifice would be too great.

Clearly Eileen had not taken independent legal advice after my brother was granted power of attorney. That Michael opted to wait until 2007 to transfer the legal title was an incredible mistake on his part – one that has had consequences for him and which he may have further cause to regret. I believe it shows an intention to relieve members of Eileen's family of their inheritance.

I was unaware of that precedent when I took up correspondence with the Police but they should have been aware of it and advised me as such.

I then wrote a letter of complaint to the Chief Constable of Hampshire Constabulary, Alex Marshall. He had previously been with Thames Valley Police - my brother's employer. I advised it appeared Hampshire Police took veiled accusations of my harassment of my step-mother earlier very seriously, going as far as involving Interpol in what could have been considered by them to have been a domestic civil case. However I did not believe they had taken my accusations as seriously against their civilian colleague, my brother.

I received a response from Detective Chief Inspector B D Snuggs of Hampshire Constabulary concerning the investigation. He reported his findings in a letter dated 30 March 2009, stating my brother's solicitors had been spoken to and claimed Eileen's will had been drawn up in accordance with instructions. [The Solicitors Regulation Authority was to disagree with that assumption at a later date].

The explanation about the missing engagement rings had also changed. Michael had initially advised they had been mislaid, then stolen, but DCI Snuggs determined there was no evidence to support my view they had been stolen, despite the fact my brother had told Ted this was the case. With reference to Eileen's bank account, that high-ranking police officer advised me Michael was 'not making an issue of this'.

Detective Chief Inspector Snuggs was, however, to provide us with valuable information – that Olive Skae was not a witness to the 2007 will signing at Belmore nursing home. This was news to Nick Jutton and I. This information was also confirmed when I eventually received a copy of the will subsequent to the issuing of the subpoena.

DCI Snuggs went on to note he believed all enquires had been undertaken, but observed they could have been conducted in a timely manner. He took the trouble of outlining the difference between suspicions and concerns and the fact he did not think they constituted evidence. In my view, it is the role of Police to seek out evidence, not members of the public.

Detective Chief Inspector Snuggs and I later talked by telephone. The conversation was lengthy and this high-ranking Police officer admitted to believing Detective Inspector Tobin made a judgment too early. More work should have been done by the original investigator.

DCI Snuggs also admitted that estates and wills provided great potential for criminal investigations. But I learned he had not even looked at a copy of the last will and at this stage he did not know the outcome of the Solicitors Regulations Authority investigation, something he could have looked into himself.

The subject of the rings was again discussed with the Police officer stating quite firmly that there were certainly suspicions around what had happened.

I brought up the subject of the Fraud Act and the failure to disclose information but these issues were skirted around. DCI Snuggs went to on say he was 'genuinely concerned' but again we came back to 'insufficient evidence'! On the matter of my father's autobiography Detective Chief Inspector Snuggs inferred that Michael would be happy to allow me to have that, but it was to take Court action and another year to actually obtain this valuable family record.

In that telephone conversation I told Detective Chief Inspector Snuggs I considered my brother to be a very dangerous, violent man, who had threatened me and that I still felt at risk. He merely indicated the best way forward for me was for me to work through my solicitor. I then asked him if he had investigated the Jersey bank account. He said he had not and would not launch any criminal investigation based on that issue.

I repeated to this senior Police officer the allegation from my brother that I had stolen money but he confirmed there was no complaint of theft against me.

Wrapping up that lengthy conversation, Detective Chief Inspector Snuggs asked if there was anything else I wanted him to do regarding my complaint against Detective Inspector Tobin. I said I would like him to investigate the issue of Eileen's Jersey bank account and he then agreed to do so, however in a subsequent email it was clear he had had a change of heart as he advised he would not sanction additional lines of enquiry.

Of course that left me once again wondering why not, as it would merely be a question of asking Michael for the information he claimed he held. In that light, I would have to question just how genuine Detective Chief Inspector Snuggs' 'genuine concerns' really were.

My suspicions that the Chief Constable's past working relationship with my brother had an effect on the investigation were also not upheld, with DCI Snuggs stating Detective Inspector Tobin had been unaware of my brother's previous employment.

~ *Thirty* ~

The intervention of DCI Snuggs had virtually crossed with my complaint to the Independent Police Complaints Commission concerning DI Tobin and subsequent to DCI Snuggs report I received a reply from that authority. I was, after all, becoming quite an expert, but the outcome was the same – the complaint was not upheld on the balance of probabilities.

However because I felt new evidence had come to light concerning this matter and having learnt from experience, I knew the next step was to make a formal complaint to Hampshire Constabulary Professional Standards Department. Detective Chief Inspector Nigel Lecointe then entered my life.

In approaching Professional Standards I added to my previous complaint by attaching further contradictory evidence which had just come into my possession. Firstly, there was the letter Eileen allegedly wrote to Rachel dated 20th July 2000 which had been produced by my brother. This was in Eileen's handwriting, but Rachel never received it and as it had been in Michael's possession, I assumed it had never been sent. In that letter Eileen stated:-

Your grandfather [Maurice Lobb] gave Adrienne the sum of £50,000 of my money without my knowledge for the purpose of looking after me financially.

A number of things were wrong with that statement. First of all, how could my father have given me money unbeknown to Eileen? She received statements of the transactions in her bank accounts, and in any event, Eileen was present when my father wrote the original cheque, as I revealed earlier in this book.

Eileen also mentioned in her diaries the Jersey bank account being in joint names and that it was made into a sole account just before my father died. I considered this letter to be defamatory but placing exculpatory evidence in the hands of the victim would have been unwise. Thus I believe that letter was never sent, instead being held for future use to plant seeds of fear in my mind – and probably Rachel's too.

Secondly, Eileen made a statement on 3rd August 2000, only a couple of weeks later, claiming that she had no knowledge of any gift, deed or assignment from her husband, Maurice Lobb, prior to his death and that I only told her about it later. My father only had the joint bank account, as recorded in Eileen's own diaries.

Thirdly, my step-mother made a statement to Hampshire Police in April 2004 stating she had informed my brother that I had taken £50,000 to look after her. In February the following year, the report from Hampshire Police indicated that £50,000 had been transferred by the late Mr Maurice Lobb to me, his daughter, in 'trust' prior to his demise.

Hampshire Police had every opportunity at that stage, while my stepmother was alive, to get to the bottom of this matter, but did not do so. Now that Eileen was dead, the story had changed.

I told the Professional Standards that my brother Michael Lobb had accused me of making my step-mother's account into a joint account and then withdrawing £54,134.24. He had told Nick Jutton and my mother this and suggested I transferred the money in 1990 so I questioned why my step-mother suddenly changed her will in 1999, nearly ten years after that actual event.

The taped conversation between my brother, my step-mother and I referred to a Jersey bank account, and the transfer of monies, not theft.

I advised Detective Chief Inspector Lecointe that this information had taken me a long time to acquire but the Police now had enough information to prosecute my brother for fraud or extortion. Unsurprisingly he concurred with Detective Chief Inspector Snuggs' conclusion that there was 'insufficient evidence' to support allegations against my brother.

My main point to the Police at that time was that my stepmother had given her apartment to my brother to compensate for him paying the debts of my father.

Detective Chief Inspector Lecointe then inquired as to whether I had asked my brother what the financial debts were that he was referring to. He suggested my brother's responses to my probe for that information would be pertinent and would shed further light on the matter and enable further assessment. Personally, I thought it was his job to find out what the debts were but he refrained from commenting on the fact that the only debts I knew about had actually been paid by me. He also wanted to know where I had obtained the information that Messrs. Edward St J Smyth had breached the solicitor's code.

This senior Police officer then advised he was going to ask one of his detective sergeants to review all the relevant material. I accepted this and to assist the process, set out specific points which I wanted to be investigated.

Two months later, I received the findings and again I was amazed, especially as no-one from the investigation had contacted me with any queries or questions.

The latest Police report observed that the cheque for £3422.16 was written on 25th November 1999 and was for repairs to 28 Richmond Court, that the cheque for £5000 – written on 9th January 2000 – was for a holiday for Eileen in Australia and that the apartment was gifted to Michael Lobb on 3rd March 2000.

The Police report then declared:

Therefore there is no deception here as the cheques were written for Eileen Lobb's property, not what is now Adrienne Nairn's brother's property. There is some argument that a further request for money by Michael Lobb to pay a bill for repairs on 30th August 2000 could be construed as cheeky as he had the apartment 'gifted' to him by this time, however Adrienne Nairn refused to pay the bill. The money for the cheques £3422.16 and £5000 was Eileen Lobb's money in any case (just being looked after by Adrienne Nairn).

I couldn't believe what I was reading. The references to a cheeky demand and theft left me amazed, once again, and showed that the Police had not grasped the simple thrust of what I was alleging.

The Police went on to note:-

Adrienne Nairn talks about handing over to her brother, Michael Lobb, a cheque for £3422.16 and a cheque for £5000 which she states was extorted from her by her brother. Extortion is a word used by Adrienne Nairn in this case. It means obtaining money in return for protection from those asking for money, usually in the form of refraining from causing damage to one's property. It is American and does not appear in English case law. There is no evidence of extortion.

The Police could not – or would not – grasp that I had repaid my father's only known debt to my brother before he had been gifted Eileen's apartment 'in consideration of the debts of Maurice Lobb.' They should have therefore been asking what other outstanding debts my father had which deemed it necessary for my step-mother to repay my brother with a £600,000 apartment?

My response was that I found the Police comments on the word 'extortion' bizarre. Extortion in my dictionary means to obtain by force, threats or unfair means, or by intimidation. Of course, I did not receive a reply.

The Police report went on to observe:-

This would appear to be where Eileen Lobb had to go on benefit because she had no money of her own. Actually Adrienne Nairn had money to the value of £50,000 which was given to her by her late father before his death in 1989 for the purpose of looking after Eileen Lobb in her later years. A tape recording has Adrienne Nairn telling Eileen Lobb to claim benefit.

My response to this is that I have never heard such a tape – it has never been produced. I would ask who was present, why was the tape made and why would I admit that when it was untrue?

More from the Police report:-

There has been a big issue made of the gift/transfer of the property of 28 Richmond Court to Michael Lobb. The first mention is by Adrienne Nairn when she accused her brother of taking advantage of an elderly vulnerable lady. This is mentioned in the letter from Scott Bailey, Solicitors dated 4th December 2008, where several documents are attached to the file including the Transfer of Registered Title document relating to 28 Richmond Court. Quote 'Our client has grave suspicions in relation to the signing by the late Mrs Lobb of her will on 21 September 2007, and the execution of the transfer document dated 18th June 2007.' The fact is that we now know that Eileen Lobb had already made a gift of her property 28 Richmond Court to Michael Lobb on 3rd March 2000, so there is no issue surrounding her giving it to him. The paperwork was the signing of the transfer, which could have been done earlier i.e. when the apartment was first gifted.

I indicated there was great issue. I initially received the copy of the title transfer document not realising the apartment had been actually gifted more than seven years previously. The Police could have found that out. It was gifted only three months after Eileen had given my brother power of attorney and no solicitor had drawn up the agreement. Eileen had not had the benefit of independent legal advice although she had used her own solicitors in Lymington only a few months previously.

The Police report also canvassed the issue of the gift from my father:-

In her statement Eileen Lobb states that in January 2000 'Adrienne gave me a cheque for £5000 and then emigrated without giving me my money back.'

The anomalies in this are obvious. On one hand, I allegedly gave Eileen her money, but on the other I refused to give her money and I emigrated in January 2000. I did not in fact emigrate until 2002, and a tape exists made in January 2000 indicating I would settle things with Eileen when I came back from our three-month world trip. But by then, it was too late. The apartment had already been gifted to Michael by then.

Another comment in that Police report was erroneous also:-

Eileen Lobb noticed that Adrienne Nairn had tried to get her bank account made joint between Adrienne Nairn and herself. [This is] something that Eileen Lobb was against.

I have to question when Eileen noticed this. My brother was to go on and say I had tried to make Eileen's bank account into a joint account. A draft letter does exist, written in a scrawl by me, because Eileen said she wanted her bank account made joint. This was not at my instigation and in any event, the account was never made joint.

Again from the Police report:-

Adrienne Nairn takes exception to this as Eileen Lobb must have known about this as she receives her bank statements. However it is known that Adrienne Nairn managed the financial affairs of Eileen Lobb up until 1999, and it is conceivable that Eileen Lobb hadn't seen the bank statements and therefore did not know of this until the taped conversation between her [Adrienne], Michael Lobb and Eileen Lobb on 9th January 2000.

Again I have to ask, how was it 'known' that I managed Eileen's financial affairs? And how was it conceivable Eileen had not seen the bank statements? They would have been sent directly to her, and those records would have been held by the bank. So why didn't the Police check?

Another point made by the Police in their report:-

Adrienne Nairn talks about a hand written will, made by someone not being her step-mother Eileen Lobb, which leaves everything to her brother. Where is this will, how does she know of its existence and whose hand does she think it is written in? Adrienne Nairn talks about witnesses and statements they have made. Who are these witnesses and where are the statements? How does she know of their existence? Adrienne Nairn talks of diaries and letters existence. How does she know they exist? Has she seen them?

Again I have to ask, why did Police not ask me these questions, rather than raising them in their investigation report? If I had copies of wills, letters and statements, they could surely have got copies themselves, and much more quickly than I obtained them. Or why did they simply not ask me to provide them before writing their report?

Subsequently I provided the following information:

Copies of the will dated 8th November 1999, the power of attorney dated 24th November 1999, the will of 28th June 2001 and the will of 21st September 2007 are all available. I have copies and Michael Lobb has copies. Ask him for them or I will provide them.

I also noted in my response to the Police report:-

The letter of 20th March 2003 is odd because it 'cancels' a will of 23rd March 1990. There was no will dated 23rd March 1990 as far as I know. There is a list written to 'Mike' dated 2nd January 2000 listing seven beneficiaries my step-mother wanted included in her will, mostly in relation to monetary bequests, but these were not included in the actual will. I wonder why? There was no will of 3rd March 2002. There is a letter dated 20th March 2003, again to 'Mike', stating 'I know you will carry out my wishes, i.e. Dawn, my niece, Alison Fletcher and Teddie Farmer.' This did not happen.

I also advised that the handwritten will existed, that I had a copy which had been forwarded by my brother's solicitors to my own, and that the Police should ask Michael for it, otherwise I could provide one. It is my view that the handwriting on that letter was that of Douggie Croshawe. I then added that the witnesses were Ted Farmer senior, Olive Corfield, Colin Beck, Alison and Mark Fletcher and Sue Humphries.

Diaries belonging to my step-mother were produced. Nick Jutton told me in November 2009 that my brother would release all my step-mother's diaries from 1986 to 2006, bar the 1990 diary which was missing and excluding the 1999 and 2005 diaries which could be photocopied and sent to him. However in an email dated the 5th January 2010 Mr Jutton said it was the 1999 and 2000 diaries which could be photocopied. This was yet another error by him.

The next segment of the Police report is extremely interesting, designated by me as such because it is untrue.

Eileen Lobb states that she was forced and manipulated to claim income support by Adrienne Nairn, who was party to Eileen Lobb claiming income support. In any event the money is Eileen Lobb's, which is being looked after by Adrienne Nairn.

The questions that flow out of this are numerous. How was I a party to Eileen being in receipt of income support? Was I ever present at any interview? Did I sign any papers? Was my name on any records? Did the Police check?

There again, if the money was indeed Eileen's, why was she in receipt of income support? But the Police didn't follow up on any of this.

The Police report contains yet another error – that 'Adrienne Nairn managed her financial affairs up until August 1999.'

The truth is that I never managed Eileen's financial affairs and there is nothing to demonstrate that I did.

The Police went on to state that the findings against Messrs Edward St J Smyth by the Solicitors Regulation Authority – which deemed them 'unprofessional' – were not 'criminal' and therefore had no bearing on a criminal investigation.

My belief is, however, that the unprofessional actions of Edward St J Smyth do have a bearing on this case, because their staff was acting on my brother's instruction not Eileen's. My brother held a power of attorney over all Eileen's affairs, but surely he did not believe that gave him the power to make Eileen's will for her or to take her apartment.

Once again I was unsurprised there was to be no further investigation of one of their colleagues. So a letter from the Hampshire Constabulary Professional Standards Department advising me of this came as no surprise. My complaint – as with all of my previous complaints – had been dismissed.

Of course there was always going to be a response from me, and there was. My subsequent letter to the Police noted:-

Mrs Lobb's blood family are backing me on this. They are not happy and have their own thoughts on my brother's actions. I am taking action because I was named as executor in Mrs Lobb's 1990 will (and Codicil) and I feel I have a duty to get to the truth. Detective Chief Inspector Snuggs certainly said he had his suspicions and if the Police have suspicions then they should be looking for the evidence – not me.

My response to what had been, effectively a re-run of previous Police decisions, went on:-

You state we differ on what I call evidence and what you call evidence. Well it is actually the job of the Police to collect the evidence and I believe you haven't even tried. You have not produced evidence of the Jersey bank account which my brother says he has. All you have to do is ask for it. This was in joint names prior to my father's death, then my step-mother made it a sole account about a week before he died. Any evidence of any debts should be there. My brother has stated that my father was bankrupt 'although undeclared' so just ask him to prove it.

The answer from DCI Lecointe:-

Unless there is a material change which leads me to believe a criminal investigation is justified, I must inform you that I am not willing to consider this any further.

I then wrote personally to Chief Constable Alex Marshall who must have worked with my brother when he was with the Thames Valley Police. I received the following reply from Inspector Kevin Baxman:-

I note your complaint and request that Mr Marshall deals with this personally. While he will be made aware of the issues raised, this is not a matter that would normally require the personal attention of the Chief Constable without the issue first being investigated by Detective Chief Inspector Lecointe's managers. Your email will be forwarded to the head of CID, Chief Superintendent Dinnell.

Detective Chief Superintendent Shirley Dinnell sat on the matter for a long time, but she finally responded, including the provision of an answer to my statement that I considered my brother to be dangerous.

I note the instigation of proceedings. I have not made the Chief Constable aware of it as this is not a matter that he would become directly involved in, as stated previously by his staff officer Inspector Baxman. I have been provided with a file of documentation and correspondence with you by Detective Chief Inspector Lecointe and I am working my way through it. I am currently unaware of any previous allegations of Mr Lobb being dangerous or of any threats or injury that he has caused you. Why have these just been raised? Having read some of the file I am not convinced that Mr Lobb does pose a physical threat to you at this time. If you have evidence that he does please contact your local Police who will risk assess the situation and provide a suitable response.

Finally I received another letter from Detective Chief Superintendent Dinnell:-

I apologise for my delay in replying to you. I am due to retire very shortly. I have had a number of outstanding things to complete and this was one of them. I can see no new information or evidence to support your allegation that a criminal offence has been committed. I am also satisfied that the Hampshire Constabulary have invested a reasonable amount of time and resources into assessing the allegations made and it is now my duty to ensure that my resources are effectively used to respond to other priorities. Consequently we will not engage in further enquiries or correspondence regarding your allegations without some significant new information.

Impending retirement and other priorities – that explained everything. The outcome was expected and again I was not surprised.

Once again however, I had been left wondering what could be more important than allegations that someone had fraudulently obtained the home of a senior citizen?

~ *Thirty One* ~

After spending £6000 with Nick Jutton for little apparent result, my pin then landed fairly and squarely on Tony Cockayne's name.

My association with Nick had been intriguing, to say the least. I found it shocking that such a failure to follow a client's instructions was not considered sufficient to even warrant a slap on the wrist. But if I thought the service provided by Nick Jutton was inadequate, I had even bigger surprises waiting.

As things turned out, Tony Cockayne of Michelmores in Exeter was to prove a far more expensive proposition. Having changed solicitors, I had to first acquaint Tony with the whole sorry saga. This took bucket loads of time, money, and energy, but I don't give up easily.

Then I get the standard advice from Tony – it is difficult to prove testamentary capacity – the legal term used to describe a person's legal and mental ability to make or alter a valid will – knowledge and approval, undue influence, fraud, transfer of property, and the prospects of success. What he did proffer also was that these cases often rested on the judge and their mood on the day, something I was already aware of.

Of course I firmly believed fraud had been committed, as did others, but Tony advised me the whole case would be touch and go. It would of course be extremely difficult to prove a case against a decorated individual too.

We got the obligatory barrister's opinion and the legal work was completed. At least Tony Cockayne did what I asked – initially. I wanted to get my brother worried and it appeared Court action was the only way to achieve that. Quite rightly, Tony and the barrister determined that some sort of mediation should take place.

Michael must have begun to get concerned because he agreed to this suggestion. Prior to the mediation, the paperwork produced by my brother was to prove interesting. Michael, for instance, referring to the scrawled draft letter I had prepared at the request of my step-mother to make her Jersey Account joint, stated it was 'likely a letter had been sent in that form', but he was awaiting confirmation from the Midland Bank.

At this stage Michael was 'relying on a handwritten entry in Eileen's diary, dated 12th April 1990, which stated 'J a/c closed – Adrienne's money'. I believe my brother was assuming 'J' stood for 'Joint' but in fact all diary entries referring to that account were Jersey – 'J' stood for 'Jersey' not 'Joint'.

In his 'defence', submitted to the Court, my brother stated:

On 12th April 1990 the sum of £54,134.24 was transferred from account number 72078465 into an account in the Claimant's sole name.

I denied this claim in my 'reply' to the Court and a 'Part 18 Request' for disclosure was made to the Court by my barrister. Surely my brother had committed an act of perjury relating an untruth in a Court document?

Michael replied as astutely as any Police officer would have, indicating to the Court he had been unable to set out the precise mechanics of the transfer of this sum and was awaiting confirmation from Jersey. Two years on, this has never been received by me and I suspect it has not been received by him either.

Michael then stated the £54,134.24 was the amount in the account on 26th July 1989, which may be correct. My father gave me the £50,000 cheque just before he died, thereby probably leaving £4134.24 in that account. My stepmother never mentioned any other figure than the £50,000, neither in any letters nor in any of the conversations with her which Michael recorded. I remain unsure, therefore, whether I was then accused of having the £50,000 in July 1989 - which I accept – as well as £54,134.24 in April 1990 – which I disagree with, or in fact both sums of money.

My brother also indicated he had no written record of me helping Eileen claim income support although he 'understood' I had. If that had actually occurred, the relevant authorities would have had a record of this. But at least Michael went on to admit, in mediation, there was no audio recording of me telling Eileen to claim such support.

I booked my flight to England, with the mediation session set down for 27th September 2010. My brother had his solicitors on hand, but what really surprised me was that he asked for his wife and my mother to attend also. By this time my mother had been moved to the Masonic Home in Exeter. I hoped they might influence him to see sense, so I agreed to their presence. This was to prove a silly decision on my part.

Most unfortunately my best ally, Ted Farmer, was out of the country, so I was attend alone.

What a terrible day that was. Long, tiring, and all but futile. Initially we sat in different rooms with our respective solicitors, me in one and Michael and his support team in the other. The mediator went from room to room relaying what had been said by each party as I had stated in no uncertain terms I was not prepared to meet my brother face to face. I had not seen this mediation session as being a mini trial and I had expected honour and a gentlemanly behaviour to prevail. Michael had no such desire, with his unfounded accusations coming thick and fast. I could not think fast enough to reply and certainly was unable to come up with the answers which would have helped had I remembered in time.

I was mindful of my elderly mother – by then 85 years of age – having to sit through all of this.

Of course I would have liked my 'fair share' of Eileen's estate, but all my brother could come up with was that we should we both walk away paying our own costs. He was not prepared to pay one single penny - not to me, nor to Rachel and in the beginning not even to her infant son Evan. I began to question what I had travelled all the way to Britain for.

I could see the mediator was becoming quite irritated by Michael's antics. He inferred to me that Penny was the driving force, and wanted to get my brother away from her. He actually took my brother for a walk around the car park to achieve this.

Eventually it was suggested I meet my brother and I was asked if I was I prepared to say sorry for what had occurred. But I had said sorry so many times to no avail that I refused. l was asked if I was I prepared to say I regretted it. I agreed –I certainly did regret what had happened.

So we all entered the mediation room. Both solicitors were there, with the mediator and Michael, who looked like thunder, but I began to say I regretted what had happened and we should try to sort everything out amicably.

Everyone in the room then turned to my brother, who, with a threatening malicious voice snarled 'I regret nothing'.

I could see the looks on the faces of both solicitors and the mediator that they were surprised by this response. In my view, my brother's behaviour that day was awful. Everyone present, I think, realised he was not going to budge, very much, if at all. I made a suggestion that a settlement be made to Rachel, but Michael vehemently refused stating 'she had my flat in London all those years ago'. She certainly rented his flat from him, which suited his requirements.

I asked for settlements for Ted Farmer's children. 'Absolutely not' was the snappy denial, before I was asked if I had known that one member of Ted's family had been 'had up for drugs'. This sharp retort took me by surprise because I did not know and could not imagine which one was being accused. Of course this came from my brother, without any evidence being produced whatsoever.

It was by then getting late. I was tired, but eventually an offer was made – Michael put forward a suggestion that £50,000 would go to Evan, my grandson, when he reached the age of 25, with that sum to be shared with any future siblings.

While I would have dearly loved my day in Court – where all the untruths would surely have been brought out into the open – my solicitor virtually begged me to accept.

I accepted, but back came the mediator with a twist – one he had never come across before - the offer from Michael had its obvious fish-hooks. He had suggested that the £50,000 for Evan would be paid in 2035, but with no interest. What would it be worth then – probably next to nothing? In the interim, Michael would continue to get the interest. I refused and the offer was reduced to £40,000, with interest, with Michael agreeing to pay it on 30th April 2011. This was for his 'tax purposes'. A 'carefully-worded' mediation order was duly drawn up.

This order makes for intriguing reading – and not only because it shows how ineffectual my solicitor was at face-to-face negotiations. First of all, the order dictated my brother must pay £40,000 into my solicitor's client account by 30th April 2011. That money was then to be invested, but agreement between Michael and I had to be reached through our respective solicitors. The beneficiaries were to be Rachel's children, who must each receive their equal share on 31st May 2035 if they survived until that date. If no children survived until that date, then the investment and any interest earned must be given to the British Legion.

The order also stipulates that if my brother and I could not reach agreement on the investment, the matter was to be taken to Court for a direction. That seems clear to lay-people, such as me, on the face of it. But what happened if either party could not, or would not negotiate agreement through their solicitor?

The mediation order also determined Michael must give my solicitor a photocopy of my late father's autobiography, although copyright ownership remained with him. This seemed to be an error as the mediator had assumed the copyright of this autobiography had passed to my brother, although there is no evidence whatsoever to establish that.

The order then went on to record that my brother must make provision in his will for Evan to be gifted named various items which had belonged to our father Maurice.

It also dictated that I must not contact my brother, sister-in-law or mother personally, via any verbal, written, electronic means, or by using any third party, unless through a solicitor or invited to.

Now, can you imagine the impossible situation my solicitor had placed me in by agreeing to this? How on earth could agreement on the investment be reached between my brother and I under such restrictive terms? He was allowed to contact me but I was not allowed to contact him!

I am certain that those with legal training – and even those without – can see these terms would be very difficult to enforce. There was, to my mind, no guarantee my grandson would receive any of the items when my brother died. They could be lost, stolen, or simply damaged, as some of Eileen's personal items had been.

After this mediation I had a meeting with Ted and Janet Farmer. They brought with them the trivia jewellery Michael had left with them. It was shameful and pitiful that Michael considered this should be all of their inheritance from Eileen.

Ted and Janet were furious at the outcome of the mediation, but there seemed little more that could be done.

My solicitor had told me that the member of the family who had 'done drugs' was young Ted's mother-in-law. In fact she was arrested the day before the wedding and therefore could not attend. I then remembered the incident as Eileen had gone to the wedding and related the story to me. She merely stated it was an embarrassment at the time and had no consequences on her relationship with young Teddy.

On my arrival back in New Zealand I wrote to my brother's solicitors stating I wished the investment of the £40,000 from Michael to be sorted long before the deadline of 30th April. I merely received a letter stating that legal firm was no longer 'instructed' by my brother.

I could already foresee problems arising.

~ *Thirty Two* ~

The 28th April 2011 fell during a weekend and holiday and true to form Michael requested a meeting with my solicitor on the very last day of that deadline week. Acting under my instructions my solicitor refused to meet him as I could not see why I should have to pay for such a discussion. In any event, the matter of the investment should have been dealt with by my brother's solicitor, who was now not under instruction and mine, who was. Surely a contravention of the order as the investment should have been made 'through our solicitors'.

At 4.30pm on 28 April 2011, my brother walked into my solicitor's office to hand over a cheque, but because of the public holiday this was not able to be banked until 3rd May, with a further few days before it was cleared. I deemed this to be another contravention of the order as cleared funds were not in my solicitor's account by the due date.

Almost two years after my brother Michael paid the funds to my solicitor, we are still awaiting a solution. I put forward two possible investment vehicles in Australia and through my solicitor, Rachel suggested a third.

All three options were declined, with Michael now demanding that the money be held in trust in one particular investment remaining untouchable until 2035. I have not agreed to this, of course, as I have seen too many people lose their money through bad investments made on their behalf. The trustees should have the power to move the funds if they see fit.

If there is one thing I agree with my brother it is that my solicitor is making hay while the sun shines. He has the money and is effectively a trustee by default, instructed by my brother. This is surely conflict of interest as the same solicitor is effectively acting on behalf of opposing parties.

Tony Cockayne of Michelmores in Exeter certainly writes letters and charges as he goes along, naturally. My own financial adviser from NatWest Bank and another from HSBC both advised me the monies could not be invested in the United Kingdom as Rachel, Evan and I are all non-residents.

Michael claimed he had provided suggestions for the investment in a letter from his financial advisers dated 12th October 2010, but neither my solicitor nor I saw a copy of this until July 2011. This did not provide specific information and nor did it not refer to the fact that our family members were not residents of the United Kingdom. This letter also stated the investment was to be in the sole name of the child. That is not possible, because the mediation order stipulated that the funds were not only for Evan, but also surviving siblings he may have when he is 25 years of age. Since his birth, Rachel has had another son, Curtis, so the mediation order is, in effect, unworkable in that regard.

Time was rolling by and in the end I concluded I had had enough of all this murky nonsense. I asked Tony Cockayne to take the matter to Court for a decision.

He refused. He wanted Counsel's advice. I did not think that was necessary, having gone through a similar exercise before. But it became evident if I did not agree Tony would then refuse to act for me.

Faced with such a prospect, I had no option but to concur so Tony put the matter before the barrister, my assumption being he would then initiate Court proceedings. However this did not happen. Tony insisted we struggle on to find an investment which would suit my brother's needs. As I felt I had already provided suitable suggestions and realising Tony was not going to carry out my instructions by taking this matter back to the Court, I took the matter into my own hands and prepared a request for direction myself. Tony Cockayne had quoted £3000 to £5000 to take this matter back to Court and I had already paid an additional £3000 on top of the original fees. I could see this escalating.

Determined to bring the matter to some form of finality, I prepared a request for a direction myself and sent it off to the Court. I thought at that time all I needed to do was then let the Court decide on the investment suggestions which I had put before it in the absence of Michael making any. In actual fact preparing the documentation took me a couple of hours and the Court costs were £80. With his superior knowledge Tony Cockayne should have done it much faster and adhered to Court procedures.

Originally I had gone to Tony Cockayne because he was a member of the Association of Contentious Trust and Probate Solicitors. Indeed he was the regional representative of that austere body and I thought he was experienced in such matters. I am afraid I seriously doubt his credentials.

By not instructing his solicitor Michael had shown an intention to delay matters, and to force me to spend more money trying to enforce the order against him.

His view was that his obligations had ceased when he made the payment to the Michelmores' client account. He also indicated he expected it to remain there until I came up with something to which he was agreeable. I couldn't believe his arrogance in indicating his intention to ignore any reasonable investment suggested by Rachel or myself.

Rachel by then was liaising with her uncle by email and advised him there was major work needed on their new house – such as fencing to make the garden safe for Evan - and a central heating/air con system. She considered both a necessity for children in the severe cold and heat of the varying seasons in Sydney. Rachel asked if she could use the funds to carry out this essential work and guaranteed to match any investment proposal my brother put forward from her own funds in 2035. What could be safer than that? In any event, if the funds were not provided to Evan in 2035 – or to any of his surviving siblings –then my brother or his legal representative would be perfectly entitled to take the matter back to Court at that time. Michael gave Rachel the impression he was considering her proposal, or would agree to it being used for Evan's education. He stated 'there's not a lot of point if Evan hasn't got the education necessary to use the money wisely'.

However this was to prove a red herring, with Michael then advising Rachel the British Legion would take on the case on his behalf because it had an interest in the outcome. I doubted this and queried it with that organisation, which subsequently advised me it would not commit itself to taking on the case, due to the uncertainty and the long timespan involved.

It would be unproductive to recount the number of letters and emails which bounced back and forth between New Zealand and the United Kingdom, but there were many. I felt Tony Cockayne hit the nail on the head by indicating he was sure my brother would not agree to anything Rachel or I suggested. As such, he conceded indicating there was no merit in getting into any protracted correspondence with my brother.

I put forward three investment suggestions to my brother, including Rachel's proposal and Michelmores hoped common sense would prevail, but in the meantime the funds remained in the client account earning a nominal interest – 0.05 per cent. Even I had not envisaged the interest was going to be that low.

Michael then advised the only thing he would agree was a bond in Evan's name, to be held under trust. However he ignored the fact that Evan's surviving siblings were to benefit too, so this could not be implemented. Two financial advisers from two separate banks had already advised me the funds could not be invested in the United Kingdom, as the beneficiaries and their parents were non-resident, so we were back to square one!

That was what drove me to commence Court action. There was to be no more naïve indecision on my part, trusting professionals to bring closure to an affair that had seemingly been going on forever. There would, I decided, be no more drowning in murky waters of deceit, compounded by professional delays and devastating tactics from my brother. Hence I set out to get a direction from the Court and that was the journey I embarked upon, with gusto and determination.

The direction hearing was set for 12th December 2011. The first setback was that the Court appeared to lose the documents. Fortunately Tony Cockayne was able to provide copies, which enabled me to put together a request for a decision. Since I was in New Zealand and the hearing was to be in Britain, it took the form of a three-way telephone conference between the judge, my brother and I.

I did not realise it was my duty to arrange for this telephone conference to be recorded until a couple of days before the hearing so Murphy's law then took hold as I went through a nerve-wracking exercise of endeavouring to set up an account with an agency in the United Kingdom.   I was told this could not be done in the time frame so set up a link from New Zealand. Fortunately for me, the judge put aside this prerequisite.

Documents then began to appear in abundance, with the revelation that my brother had advised the Court I had a criminal record – in that a harassment order had been served on me.

It was of course simple enough for me to prove such an order had never been served, but one could not help but wonder what Michael's motive was for putting that before the Court. In my view, all he risked doing was confirming to the judge that he was prone to misrepresenting the facts – intentionally, recklessly, or carelessly.

I had asked the Court for a direction as to the investment of the funds and provided it with two suggested investment vehicles. The third option was that Rachel be permitted to use the funds for improvements to the house, thereby benefiting Evan and any future siblings. I also asked the Court to confirm I had put the suggested investment vehicles in an acceptable format and what the fee would be, but received no reply.

As something of a booby prize perhaps, I was notified my brother had been given leave to attend the hearing in person, contravening the arrangement for a three-way telephone conference. Of course I objected because I felt this would give him an unfair advantage and his approval to attend in person was reversed by the Court.

Eventually the day of the telephone conference arrived and while it was day-time in England, it was late night in New Zealand. I am never very good that late in the evening.

The Court hearing did not begin well – lo and behold, Michael was in attendance in flesh and blood. He claimed he had not received any notification of the reversal and when questioned by the judge he inferred he had to attend because he had to wear hearing aids. This was the first time I had ever heard of such an infliction! But in an effort to obtain some sort of progress, I agreed for the hearing to go ahead with my brother in attendance.

Judge Britton was on the Bench and from the outset he insisted issues relating to procedure had to be addressed.

The first hurdle was that the Judge indicated the hearing by telephone had not been set up in accordance with Court rules, which stipulated they must only be recorded by authorised service providers.

The next procedural problem was my request for a decision. The Judge said if a Court order was being sought it must be applied for in England or Wales, using a claim form. However he did agree to treat my request for a decision as a formal application but that required a fee of £80 to first be paid.

Finally Judge Britton went on to clearly indicate he would have great difficulty making any decision on the basis of the documentation because none of it actually detailed any investment vehicles. This was peculiar as I had provided full details of the two suggested investments vehicles and my brother had confirmed he had received copies of them. The Judge however did not appear to have them in his file, although they were listed as attachments, so he adjourned the hearing and formulated an order on the spot.

I was, of course, ordered to pay the £80 Court fee, which I was perfectly happy to do and would have done so previously if I had been advised of the amount.

What undoubtedly was my biggest success was that Judge Britton ruled that in the normal course of events the law would allow the income to be used for the benefit of the beneficiaries, but the difficulty was my brother would not agree to that. The Judge also made comment that my brother wanted the funds to be locked away in one specific investment for the whole term. The Judge conceded this was incorrect, in the sense of the term of the schedule which said it must be invested for the benefit of the children and to be distributed to those surviving in 2035. That did not automatically mean the funds must be locked up for the entire time or in one investment, indeed it would be difficult to find an investment which was guaranteed to be around in 2035. The Judge also went on to say it was not necessarily the case that the funds could not be invested outside the United Kingdom. I was now also able to contact Michael directly regarding the issues raised.

By then however my own money was beginning to run low after paying vast sums to solicitors. As my brother indicated, these legal boffins had obtained around fifty per cent more from us both in fees than the total amount of the fund in question.

While Judge Britton's ruling did provide me with a partial victory over my brother, I had major difficulties with his approach. He took no interest at all in the fact that the mediation order had not been adhered to with the monies being late, insisting that this was of no consequence at that stage. The Judge also could not initially see that both parties were supposed to use their solicitors to agree on the investment and investment vehicles. I had, of course, used my solicitor whilst my brother had not.

But it is true I was especially pleased Judge Britton at least declared that the £40,000 should not be locked in one investment for another 24 years.

One major problem remained, however, that of getting Michael to give me consent to contact his financial advisor to obtain details of the investment vehicle proposed on his behalf.

The mediation order barred me from contacting Davidsons, my brother's financial advisor, so I asked the Judge if I may do so. It seemed crucial to me that we use one financial adviser otherwise we would again be in a state of limbo. However that was not forthcoming. Judge Britton would not grant me access to liaise and did not ask my brother for his consent. Instead, he indicated I should write to Michael seeking his approval, or to appoint my own financial advisor to seek this from him. To employ two financial advisers who would come up with two investment strategies seemed pointless to me when I would have been perfectly prepared to accept any suitable investment vehicle if only I were allowed to ask my own questions.

Judge Britton went on to indicate that my brother was unlikely to give consent since he had refused in the past. Why he simply did not ask my brother there and then, or override the very strict mediation order condition remains a mystery to me. But he did not and he then concluded the hearing.

It seemed that the war which had begun so many years before was destined to go on.

~ *Thirty Three* ~

My first action after the hearing was to write to Tony Cockayne and tell him of my dissatisfaction. If he had taken the matter to Court in May as I requested, he would hopefully have followed the correct procedures, and ensured the suggested investment vehicles had been received by the Court.

I threatened to report him to the Legal Ombudsman, which prompted intervention from the senior partner, Will Michelmore. He endeavoured to find a solution to the problem, eventually coming up with the concept of a trust bond, with himself and me as trustees. On the face of it this was entirely acceptable to me, but true to form my brother put a spanner in the works, insisting that he be a trustee and refusing to accept me. So we were effectively thrust into another stalemate by Michael.

My brother was at that stage still refusing to instruct his own solicitor, but he had no hesitation in contacting Will Michelmore directly. Clearly my solicitor should not have been taking any instructions from my brother.

My complaint about the level of interest the fund was attracting led to a suggestion that the investment money be placed in a National Savings Account attracting one and three quarters per cent and to my surprise, Michael agreed with this. But months on, this has not been implemented and when I asked why not, Will Michelmore advised me he was still waiting for written consent to do so.

Michael had in fact advised that while he was supportive of the transfer in principal, he thought it would be a waste of time and effort since he expected agreement on the investment vehicle in the short-term. That was a very clever tactic on my brother's part.

By mid-January 2012 I had grown tired of Michelmores continual refusals to give me copies of the correspondence between themselves and my brother. Judge Britton had, after all, indicated than non-disclosure only led to confusion between the parties to say the least. In an effort to avoid the mistrust deepening, I instructed Michelmores not to contact my brother any further – at least until I received copies of all his correspondence. I also insisted that the investments funds be placed in a National Savings account immediately as I did not want any more money to be lost or any more costs to be incurred and I certainly did not want any further delay on obtaining closure on the mediation order.

Will Michelmore responded by indicating he was again requesting the consent from my brother he believed was required to transfer the funds and he insisted my brother and myself must agree in principle to form a trust in England. Although Will Michelmore advised he had sourced a trust which might be agreeable to both my brother and I, he refused to tell me the name of the provider. After 12 months of inaction, I was furious.

Michael continued to delay the process, firstly ignoring my suggestion that Rachel ought to be the trustee, then suggesting our cousin Madeleine fill this role as she was my daughter's godmother. Michael also suggested our mother's solicitor, David Burnett, be appointed due to that lawyer being 'impartial, trustworthy, and an excellent judge of character, besides being a close friend of the family.' Impartial and a close friend of the family - I don't think so. He was certainly not my friend, after all he had written to my mother advising her he thought I had a mental problem.

Michael went on to suggest that Iain Bryce would listen to all sides of the story before then making any decisions, that he had extensive experience as an ex-director of Ernst Young, had well-proven probity, and would remain loyal as a family friend of many decades. But I remembered my brief meeting with Iain Bryce and his scathing oral outburst on that occasion in Bridlington, during which I perceived he believed the ridiculous accusations made by my brother and mother – none of which had any foundation. However I wrote to both Madeleine and Iain Bryce for their confirmation they were happy to be trustees. Neither of them bothered to reply.

Finally Michael put up Michelmores as a trustee, but my faith in that legal firm had by then been well and truly eroded.

The path to the Legal Ombudsman seemed desirable by then and as it turned out, I did not have to wait long for a decision. My complaint was accepted on 1st February 2012 and I received the decision exactly a month later. The Ombudsman found as follows:-

The complainant has stated the solicitors did not act upon the fact the Court order was broken in that the funds were not paid on time. I cannot see that this was a service the firm has agreed to act on. The money was paid on time.

This is contrary to the facts – the money certainly was not paid on time! But the Ombudsman went on:-

> The firm explained why they were not able to apply to the Court. This was because the duty they owed to the Court overrides the duty to follow the complainant's instructions to take the matter back to Court. The Court has given clear directions as to how the matter needs to be taken forward. It does not involve the firm at all. The firm have explained they do not wish to act for the complainant on dealing with this. This is because the lawyer/client relationship is broken. If the complainant wants legal help to bring the matter back before the Court then it is necessary to instruct different lawyers. I cannot see poor service by the firm.

My comment on this is that I paid that law firm £3000 to take the matter back to Court and it was happy to take my money. I certainly felt that firm was involved, after all it had drawn up the Court Order. Further from the Ombudsman:-

> The firm is not providing a legal service by holding the monies on account. The firm is in effect interim trustee, awaiting further instructions from the complainant and her brother. I cannot look at complaints about the firm not moving money to a different account.

So Michelmores was now deemed to be the interim trustees. If so, surely its duty was to do its best for the beneficiaries? On the one hand it was awaiting instructions from my brother and I, and on the other it did not follow instructions to move the funds to a different account. I had agreed and my brother had agreed in principle. The Ombudsman then went on further:-

> In relation to the failure by the firm to forward correspondence, whether there is poor service depends on what capacity the firm received the correspondence. If this correspondence was received by the firm when acting for the complainant in resolving a dispute with her brother it should be forwarded.

Clearly Michelmores had received the correspondence when acting for me in trying to resolve the dispute. The next part of the Ombudsman's ruling stated:-

> However my view is that the correspondence has been received by the firm in its capacity as an interim trustee. As such it cannot forward the letters without the consent of the sender. This is so in order to treat each party fairly and equally.

As it stands both my brother and I need to agree together on the investment of this money – the trustees are answerable to us both. On this basis it would hardly be fair for them to carry on a correspondence with just one party? But in any event, the Ombudsman continued:-

> The complainant says she cannot supply names of trustees without details of the proposed investment. I do not consider the firm are providing a legal service. The firm, as an interim trustee, has merely pointed out that to move matters forward the first step is for the complainant and the brother to agree trustees who could then take over the investment from the firm and act in accordance with a trust deed that the firm is willing to draft.

I made my complaint to the Ombudsman on 1st February 2012. Michelmores advised in a letter dated 3rd February 2012 it was no longer prepared to act for me, but at the date of my complaint that firm was still providing a legal service to me. Michelmores invoiced me and I paid this. So the Ombudsman was taking facts into account which didn't exist at the time of my complaint:-

> I note that the complainant now agrees to the firm writing to her brother for consent on various matters. This is of no use as the firm has said it is no longer willing to act. The Court order the complainant obtained in December 2011 made clear what steps needed to be taken. If the complainant needs legal help to take these steps then a different firm will need to be instructed.

The original Court order stated the monies were to be invested through the law firms acting for me and my brother. My solicitors were Michelmores, which wrote itself into the agreement, then refused to act!
The Ombudsman concluded his formal finding with the following:-

For all the above reasons I consider no remedy is required and in all the circumstances of this case that is fair and reasonable.

No further recourse on that ruling is available, but that does not mean I have to be happy with it. Clearly I am not.

Michael's intentions seemed very clear, to me anyway, and I now felt I had no option but to appoint yet another solicitor to take the matter back to Court or to represent myself again based on the investment vehicles I proposed originally.

Years had passed and while Michael had paid £40,000 into a client account of a legal firm in the United Kingdom, I was no further forward in getting the benefits of that transferred to my grandson, who by now had been joined by a sibling.

~ *Thirty Four* ~

For a little while Michael continued to have email correspondence with Rachel. It took two forms.

One was the investment matter, whereby Rachel tried her best to bring this matter to a speedy conclusion for the sake of her children – to no avail – and the other was the more personal communications.

Given these, it is easy for me to reflect on how my brother has been faring through the years, particularly in the context of my incredible argument with Eileen and Michael's innermost thoughts on various subjects.

After a ten-day day break in the Azores he once proffered that he enjoyed spending his wealth on holidays. This particular one had been a good holiday. He had not spoken Portuguese for twenty years, but it flooded back in chunks, clearly indicating he suffered no memory loss over the years.

Holidays have abounded for him and his wife Penny – a sea journey around Scotland, trips to Vietnam and Cambodia, and yet another tiger expedition to India. By all accounts, he was doing well and he loved the power and prestige wealth brought him.

An example of that wealth is the five such heirloom clocks. One was the Nathaniel Birt clock he acquired on Mother's move to Devon. It stood to the left of the fireplace in the Bridlington dining room and has a religious cross displayed prominently on the front of the case. Nathaniel Birt was a London based clock-maker who manufactured the clock in 1690. As well as the clocks my brother has stated between them, he and my cousin Madeleine, own seven houses. Both are Rachel's godparents and neither have children.

My father had mentioned the Lobb heirlooms and he set out his wishes for what should happen to these in his autobiography. His memoirs mentioned a tankard which Michael subsequently had professionally assessed. He claims this was of minimal value, despite it probably being produced in the early eighteenth century. I remember this tankard well as it was always to come to me. There was a little note inside in my father's handwriting stating 'For Adrienne' but of course I never got it. It was of no consequence to me that it was worthless as my father wanted me to have it, along with other items obviously.

Another such heirloom was my grandfather's watch with Prince Albert chain and five point star emblem. Our father kept it displayed in a cabinet as Michael was roaming the world with the army. He was livid when my father gave it to Eileen, but he went on to tell Rachel.

She wore it to the day she died and it gave her a lot of pleasure. She didn't have much.

Michael now wears it with evening dress and considers it an heirloom he will keep in the family, as is the case with the Woodsmansey album and Bible.

The items now in Michael's possession will remain with him, I am sure. He has indicated an intention to keep them in the family and has inferred he will leave them to Rachel's children – on the condition no-one rocks the boat. I suspect that comment is aimed at me! He has suggested the medals will go to the RTR Museum at Bovington or the SAS at Hereford.

He has indicated he can see no reason whatsoever why he should not consider that all my father's memorabilia should go to his great nephews, but reiterated this depends on the behaviour of 'certain people'. These days there are a lot of ambiguous comments being tossed around, leaving me to conclude that not only did my brother learn the art of killing and survival with the Special Air Services, but also the literary art of deceit. It is unfortunate the army did not teach him family values instead of training any semblance of empathy out of him. To me it looks like we must all behave ourselves, according to Michael's wishes, if my grandchildren are to get what is actually due to them by law. He clearly relishes being in control.

My brother was awarded an MBE in 2002 for services to the Police and he has strong views on this honour and also the etiquette surrounding it. He was most displeased with Rachel for not congratulating him at that time. He is very patriotic and considers it an insult not to recognise any honour given by Her Majesty the Queen of England. His displeasure is difficult to understand as he did not tell Rachel of his MBE.

According to him it was for Rachel's parents to announce such events as weddings, births, Queen's honours and the like. In my view this is utter nonsense.

I have always viewed Michael's MBE with a degree of disdain - the usual gongs for the boys, no more and no less. He was employed by the Police and merely did what he was paid to do. What he did to earn such an honour escapes me.

I used to be proud of my brother Michael, my only sibling, but I do not have that feeling of admiration now. Too much water has passed under the bridge and I have seen too much of his dark side to be comfortable with the person he has become.

Times change. We all know that and I believe if my brother had any children of his own - and then grandchildren – he would have moved with the times, as people do.

In my view, Michael displays a somewhat confused view on our roots, where our family came from and where it is going. He believes we are only what we make ourselves, but almost in the same breath points out that Rachel is fifty per cent a Lobb, whereas her son Evan is only twenty five per cent.

Michael appears proud of what he made himself. He has often boasted about how he did 25 years in the army, compared with our father's six years of service. He ignores the war scenario and Dad's part in it, or the fact he was wounded in France, had to be evacuated and suffered the rest of his life as result of those injuries. In my mind, there was no comparison between my father's army service and my brother's. My father fought for his country in the Second World War, but my brother had no such bloody open warfare honour – he finished his career as a highly-paid mercenary!

Although 'retired' he still lectures on military subjects. He was at Balliol College (Oxford) with American Special Forces and in Ireland talking to troops going to Afghanistan. He classifies that as being 'worthwhile'.

The military organisations to which he belongs keep him more than busy. Most involved are welfare cases. 'Ex-servicemen fallen on hard times. It is very sad. Can't say I enjoy that aspect very much but – as they say – someone has to do it'.

He is Rachel's godfather, but I often wonder if there is really any need to remind her that she must conform to his rigid wishes in order to inherit some of his wealth in the future. My brother is good at creating illusions of doing tremendous favours through the psychology of who dares wins.

He also wields a confused view on respect for the elderly, saying on one hand that these folk should not be placed in vulnerable positions, as he felt the Queen was during her recent visit to Northern Ireland. But on the other hand he clearly had no such respect for Eileen, when he set about breaking up the excellent relationship I had with her. In my view Michael had little respect for Mother also, destroying her relationship with her daughter, her grand-daughter and great-grandsons. I will never forgive him for making our Mother – at 85 years of age – sit through a lengthy, horrendous mediation process, which drained me, a woman in my early sixties.

So what of Ian and I? How have we fared since settling down in New Zealand? I can say that after the long saga with Eileen, there have been no regrets about our decision to move here. Sibling rivalry I could take and innuendo I could handle, but lies which had no foundation I simply could not bear, particularly the defamation of our father by claiming he had died with such a degree of debt that Michael was entitled to take a £600,000 penthouse apartment as compensation!

We love it in Taupo, New Zealand. We have settled into the life extremely well, making many friends and I enjoy my voluntary work. We love our small house too, with its magnificent views of the great lake and distant mountains, a view many visitors say is worth a million dollars.

I do often dwell however on what might have been. Had I received what really should have been my share of Eileen's penthouse apartment things might have been very different. The fight I have been embarking on is just for me, Ian, Rachel or her children. Eileen's niece and nephew were originally named as pecuniary beneficiaries. Eileen's second cousins, Alison, Susan and Ted Farmer should have also been beneficiaries, as she had originally intended. Their inheritance would have really meant a lot, and been so helpful.

As life draws on, I believe many lessons could be learned by my brother Michael. For all his army training I know he is not brave enough to utter the hardest word in the world – sorry.

Michael should never have involved himself in the tiff between Eileen and I. He has stated he has been involved in two reconciliation processes – in Northern Ireland where he dealt with Protestant victims of the IRA atrocities, and in Namibia between the black workforce and white management in the diamond mines. This is scary stuff considering that he cannot work through his own family problems and in fact exacerbated them.

Today the life Ian and I have is not without its pleasures or treats. We occasionally have breaks, particularly on special occasions. For Ian's seventieth birthday we had a wonderful cruise around the Marlborough Sounds with Rachel and Jamie, then to a special night in a special place. We set off on exciting outback adventures too as often as we can, although we mainly travel to exhilarating short-break destinations. Naturally we also travel to Sydney often.

Quite recently a great thing happened. Ian had been married before I met him and had four children. The youngest, Barbara, died of leukaemia just before her third birthday. His three other children were Robert, the eldest, Linda and Pam.

Unfortunately, Ian had lost contact with the children when his marriage broke down and with us living in England for so long probably did not help. We did, however, think about them often and had tried tracing them but without result.

Then one day, a man was standing in a long queue at the local hardware store in Auckland. He decided to switch to another line as it was shorter and fate intervened as he was served by a young friend of ours, James, who recognised the name and through him, we were able to reconnect with Ian's son, and then with Linda and Pam. There have been no recriminations, just lots of laughter and we have met Ian's three grandchildren and two great grandchildren.

As things stand, this story is by no means over. An autobiography, in effect is never really over until death. But when that time comes, it would be nice to know you did your best in life, made every effort to sort out any problems – to put them behind you and move on. I believe I have always tried to do my best for people and to be a good friend.

I would not like to depart this earth leaving unsolved problems and unfinished matters. In many respects, I am like my father – a fighter who stood up for his rights. It's a shame really, how power is actually designed to be abused by those who wield knowledge, leaving their victims with no choice but to trust them until too late. In my view it is even worse when those with such power are decorated and are supposed to be looking after the interests of family members.

My experiences over the last thirteen years have demonstrated to me that it is a quite a soul-destroying exercise to fight such people, but we must battle on, to hold on to my sanity if nothing else.

Committing these facts and thoughts to paper in this way has helped immensely too. My conscience is clear and my hellish nightmares have ceased to haunt me. I can now wake up in the mornings feeling I have had a good sleep.

If my own problems with my brother are not sorted, I do hope this book will at least bring to the fore the issues that can arise in the circumstances in which I have found myself, and which many others do also within family affairs.

I do not believe it is right that someone can take an elderly woman's home in such a manner. To my way of thinking, a law change is required in the United Kingdom to ensure that any such granted power must be registered from the onset. The donor of the property must by law have separate legal advice or if mentally incapacitated then the consent of at least two members of the grantor's family should be obtained.

Will politicians agree, or even look at this pressing issue? Statutory law is formulated on their say so, but they can override common law if they so choose. The jury remains out on whether anyone in Britain's Parliament has the courage to take such a step.

When I first started writing this book it was dedicated to Evan, who bounced into this world on the 31st May 2010. Future generations, hopefully, will go on. That is one reason I felt I had to put my family story into print. We love you Evan - you are funny, adorable, loving and give us hours of entertainment.

Now you have a brother. On 10th May 2012 we welcomed Curtis, our second grandson into this world. He is also healthy, gorgeous and raring to go. The only settlement your great uncle Michael was prepared to make at the mediation was in your names and any future siblings. But now almost two years later it sits languishing in a solicitors' account bearing only minimal interest. Those earnings could be so much more but for the unreasonable controlling behaviour of your great uncle. Your Poppa, Ian, always said: 'Never expect anything in this life and you will not be disappointed.' These were very wise words indeed.

What I want to say to Evan and Curtis is that you can expect and will receive all your parents' love, with the same from Ian and I. You may not inherit the family fortunes, heirlooms, or your great grandfather's cups and medals, but you can be assured that health, love and happiness means much more than money and you have those in abundance.

~ *Appendices*~

~ *Appendices* ~

"Letter of Authority" to
make Eileen's a/c joint.

30.9.89

Dear Sirs
High Interest Cheque
A/c No. 720784405,
E. M. COBB.

I should be pleased if
you would make the
above a/c joint with
her daughter MRS
Adrienne Nairn of
66 Sambrook
L——.

A spec. of her signature
appears below.

Diary notes Re: Jersey bank account and insurance March 1987

5 Thursday 'Phone Bernard. + Mottie.
Drew money from P.O. Pay into Midland Bank, Worthing
£8,856. for Jersey.
Cash & Carry.

July 1989

Wednesday 19

Tim coming here — Did not come.
Michael. ✓
Wrote to Midland Bank Jersey putting money
into my name only — was joint A/c.

Thursday 20

Perm H/c. Cancelled Mottie too ill

January 2006

9 Monday   "Go To Bank" —
sort out my A/c. —
Have been paying twice for HOME CONTENTS

214

Dairy notes Re: Jersey bank account 1990

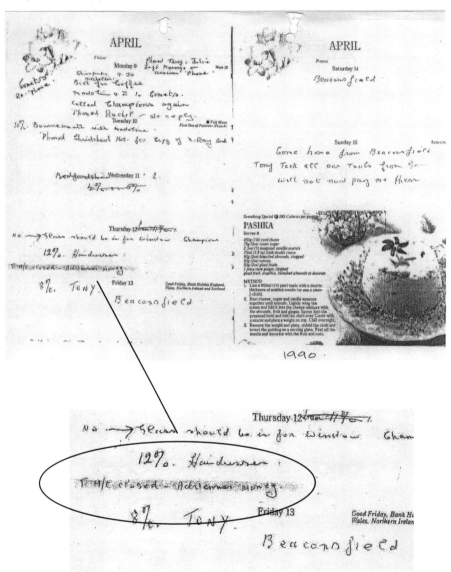

Note of Thursday 12th reads
- J A/c closed Adrienne's money -

Cheque for £5000 for Eileen to go to Australia

Cheque for £3422.16 to my brother repaying only known debt left by my father.

Eileen's wishes relayed to my brother concerning pecuniary bequests.
This instruction was not carried out.

To MIKE - MY STEPSON —   2-1-2000.
    Lobb

P/A.   MY WILL.

My brother in Law   —   William Tate. 44. Balthorpe Gardens
  £5,000 .   Sutton . Surrey.

1. Cousin :-   Alison Mary Farmer   4 Page Hill Avenue.
  £5,000.   Buckingham.

                        Susan Elizabeth Farmer
£ 5,000   4. Page Hill Avn. Buckingham.

£ 5. 000   Edward Farmer Junior .
                        4 Page Hill Avn. Buckingham.

my niece
10, 000.   Dawn Boden . 33. Sutherland Avn.
                        Yate . Bristol.

My Nephew .
5. 000 .   Nigel Tate . 32. St. Theresa's Close.
                        Havant. Hampshire .

ends. My/   Terence & Julia Herbert. 42. Cardinal Ct.
of Plated Cutlery Set Grand Avenue. Worthing – W. Sussex.
nton Dinner Service.

                        Eileen Mary Lobb.

217

Extracts from Eileen's medical notes.

30.1.2006
G.P.Surgery
Dr Lucy Joseph

      S: Main concern is memory. Feels it is poor. No
         relatives to give collateral history. ? hoew long
         this has been going on for. Mood low
         intermittently. No psychoses. Sleeping well.
         Appetite poor longterm. MMSE 24/30. For bloods and
         Becton referral.

1.5.2006   End
.P.Surgery
rs Catherine Rose

      E: C/O - wax in ear
      O: c/o blocked lt ear,no wax in canal,drum looks
         cloudy.Says she can hear herself breathing,has not
         got normal hearing.
      D: Says she feels v.depressed,has great difficulty
         getting out chair and walking.Is breathless and
         oedema+++,not taking diuretics again.
         Glucose 6.5 mmol/l will ask Social worker to call
         to assess

30.11.2006
Home Visit
Dr C F SEWARD

      S: not eating ? nausea. Poor comprehension and
         memory. Leg swelling still, circulatory, says
         keeps them up but evidence suggests otherwise.
         Some excoriations but not too bad
     Rx: Domperidone Tablets 10 mg
      T: White British Ex-moderate smoker (10-19/day)

8.11.2006
Home Visit
Dr C F SEWARD

      S: ex hosp, back pain, giddy and depressed
     Rx: Tramadol Hydrochloride Capsules 50 mg
         Temazepam Tablets 10 mg
         Stugeron Tablets 15 mg
      D: Medication review with patient

11.4.2007
Home Visit
Dr C F SEWARD

      S: SOB still, not taking tabs or keeping feet up.
         advised to take meds, also check bloods re
         medications
      O: chest clear
      P: discussed with carers her lack of compliance with
         recommendations or medications. Is not taking tabs
         as prescribed at all

Further extracts from Eileen's medical notes

Patient No:22849 Mrs Eileen M Lobb Page - 12 of 37

```
                                              Fordingbridge hospital - sc.
                                              23.7.07.(
                                              DischargesummaryFordingbridgeho
                                              spitalsc23707.tif)
23.08.2007 Patient File Attachment           :Discharge summary G7 SGH - 3
                                              pages sc. 29.8.07.(
                                              DischargesummaryG7SGH3pagessc29
                                              807.tif)
24.08.2007 Patient File Attachment           :Discharge from Hythe hospital -
                                              sc. 9.9.07.(
                                              DischargefromHythehospitalsc990
                                              7.tif)
04.09.2007 Patient File Attachment           :Spell summary Lymington
                                              hospital - sc. 9.9.07.(
                                              SpellsummaryLymingtonhospitalsc
                                              9907.tif)
05.09.2007 Patient File Attachment           :Discharge summary Hythe
                                              Hospital - sc 060907(
                                              DischargesummaryHytheHospitalsc
                                              060907.tif)
21.09.2007 Nursing/other home                :
14.11.2007 Influenza vaccination             :Home Visit, B9683-1 exp 6/08
-------------------------------------------------------------------------
All consultations
```

```
13.12.2007
Path. Lab.
Dr Angela SIZER
            I: Urine microscopy, Urine culture (*R16)


3.10.2007
Path. Lab.
Dr Angela SIZER
            I: !Urine microscopy, Urine culture, Urine
               culture, Sample: organism sensitivity
               (*R15)


6.9.2007          Review
ome Visit
r Angela SIZER
            E: [Congestive cardiac failure ] replaced with Left
               ventricular failure
            S: feels very low and tearful.
               sleep not too bad but miserable, staff concerned.
            O: depressed, tearful, forgetful, no interest,
               putting on brave face,
           Rx: Sertraline Hydrochloride Tablets 50 mg


1.9.2007
elephone
: D E READ
            S: redness swelling lt foot
           Rx: Flucloxacillin Capsules 500 mg
```